1001 Yiddish Proverbs

1001
Yiddish
Proverbs

FRED KOGOS

A Citadel Press Book
Published by Carol Publishing Group

First Carol Publishing Group Edition 1990

Copyright © 1970 by Fred Kogas

A Citadel Press Book
Published by Carol Publishing Group

Editorial Offices
600 Madison Avenue
New York, NY 10022

Sales & Distribution Offices
120 Enterprise Avenue
Secaucus, NJ 07094

In Canada: Musson Book Company
A division of General Publishing Co. Limited
Don Mills, Ontario

Manufactured in the United States of America
ISBN 0-8065-0455-2

10 9 8 7 6 5 4 3

This book is dedicated to my wife
Sarah Pollock Kogos
for her patience and understanding,
her constant assistance
her everlasting encouragement,
and her enduring love

Introduction

MY STUDY of Yiddish proverbs has proved to be a fascinating and intriguing adventure. The fabric of Jewish proverbial wisdom woven over the centuries now has become a magnificent tapestry of maxims, aphorisms, and pithy sayings reflecting the devious course of Jewish history. In it can be described the longings and strivings, the trials and tribulations, the joys and griefs of the Jewish people.

Yiddish proverbs deal with many subjects, ranging from the homely happenings of everyday life to man's highest aspirations; they mirror the philosophy, wisdom, and culture that safeguarded the Jews' sanity and preserved their identity through millennia of suffering, affliction, expropriation, expulsion, persecution and holocaust.

The Jews ridiculed themselves and others in their proverbs, they rejoiced over glad tidings, and they hid their grief in the face of adversity. The proverbs were a mask, a crutch, a guidepost, a hope. They reveal the warmth of a people and, above all, their indominatable humor, well expressed in the proverb, "Suffering makes you laugh too."

Yiddish proverbs are usually restrained and gentle in their satire. They represent a seeking for social standards, a search for spiritual insights and ethical solutions to human conduct. In their proverbial wisdom the Jews also reveal great understanding of psychology. As Dr. A. A. Roback has said, the Jews had to become psychologists, of course, for it improved their chances of survival!

In the words of the Holy Bible, "Acquaint thyself with proverbs, for of them thou shalt learn instruction."

FRED KOGOS

PRONUNCIATION GUIDE

VOWELS

a as in f*a*ther
i as in l*i*t
e as in b*e*d
o as in h*o*t
u as in p*u*t

DIPHTHONGS

ai as in s*ay* or m*ai*n
ei as in b*y* or h*ei*ght
oi or *oy* as in b*oy* or v*oi*ce
(When two other vowels appear together, pronounce them separately.)

CONSONANTS

dz as in soun*ds*
g as in *g*o
ch as in lo*ch* or Ba*ch*
r soft (no trill)
ts as in pa*ts*
tsh or *tch* as in *ch*urch
zh as in sei*z*ure

AS TO ACCENT

In words of two syllables, the accent usually falls on the first syllable. In words of three syllables or more, the accent usually falls on the second syllable. Words elongated by prefixes or suffixes retain the original accent. (I hope that is not too *ongepatchket* [muddled] for you!)

1001 Yiddish Proverbs

1

A badchen macht alemen frailech un alain ligt er in drerd.

The wedding jester makes everyone laugh; he alone is miserable.

2

A baizeh tsung iz erger fun a shlechter hant.

A wicked tongue is worse than an evil hand.

3

A barg mit a barg kennen zich nit tsuzamen kumen, ober a mentsh mit a mentsh kennen.

Mountains cannot meet, but men can.

4

A behaimeh hot a langen tsung un ken kain brocheh nit zogen.
An animal has a long tongue, yet he can't recite a blessing.

5

A behaimeh hot a langen tsung un ken nisht reden; der mentsh
hot a kurtseh un tor nisht reden.
*Animals have long tongues but can't speak; men have short
tongues and shouldn't speak.*

6

A bisseleh chain iz shoin nit gemain.
A little charm and you are not ordinary.

7

A bitter hartz redt a sach.
An embittered heart talks a lot.

8

A bocher a shadchen, a moid a bobbeh—konnen nisht zein.
*A bachelor a matchmaker, a spinster a grandmother—these
cannot be.*

9

A chissoren, di kalleh iz tsu shain.
A fault-finder complains even that the bride is too pretty.

10

A chossen a yaden gait nit on naden.
You can't have a learned bridegroom without a dowry.

11
A dank ken men in kesheneh nit legen.
You can't put "thank you" in your pocket.

12
A dokter un a kvores-man zeinen shutfim.
Doctors and gravediggers are partners.

13
A falsheh matba'ieh farliert men nit.
A bad penny always turns up.

14
A farshporer iz besser vi a fardiner.
A saver is better than an earner.

15
A foilen iz gut tsu shiken nochen malech-hamoves.
It's a good idea to send a lazy man for the Angel of Death.

16
A freint bekamt men umzist; a soineh muz men zich koifen.
A friend you get for nothing; an enemy has to be bought.

17
A freint bleibt a freint biz di kesheneh.
A friend remains a friend up to his pocket.

18

A freint darf men zich koifen; sonem krigt men umzist.

A friend you have to buy; enemies you get for nothing.

19

A fremdeh tsoreh iz kain tsibeleh nit vert.

The troubles of a stranger aren't worth an onion.

20

A fremdeh bissen shmekt zis.

Another man's tidbit smells sweet.

21

A fremdeh pelz varemt nit.

Another's cloak does not keep you warm.

22

A fremder nar iz a gelechter; an aigener—a shand.

A strange fool is a laughing stock; your own—a shame.

23

A froi, zogt men bei undz, hot langeh hor un kurtsen saichel.

A woman, they say, has long hair and short sense.

24

A gast iz vi regen az er doi'ert tsu lang, vert er a last.

A guest is like rain: when he lingers on, he becomes a nuisance.

25

A ganef fun a ganef iz potter.
It's no crime to steal from a thief.

26

A gelechter hert men veiter vi a gevain.
Laughter is heard farther than weeping.

27

A gemachteh machashaifeh iz erger fun a geborener.
A woman turned witch is worse than one who is born so.

28

A geshvir iz a guteh zach bei yenem untern orem.
A boil is fine as long as it's under someone else's arm.

29

A guteh tochter iz a guteh shnur.
A good daughter makes a good daughter-in-law.

30

A guten helft a vort; a shlechten helft afileh kain shteken oich nit.
A word helps a good person; but even a stick can't help the bad.

31

A guten vet der shaink nit kalyeh machen, un a shlechten vet der bes-hamedresh nit farichten.
A good man can't be corrupted by the tavern nor a bad one reformed by the synagogue.

32

A guter freint iz oft besser fun a bruder.
A good friend is often better than a brother.

33

A guter vort iz karanter fun a nedoveh.
A kind word is better than alms.

34

A guter Yid darf nit kain briv, a shlechten Yidden helft nit kain briv.
A good person doesn't need a letter of recommendation; for a bad one, it would do no good.

35

A halber emes iz a gantser ligen.
A half truth is a whole lie.

36

A halber entfer zogt oichet epes.
Half an answer also says something.

37

A halber nar iz a gantser chochem.
A half-fool is a very wise man.

38

A hartz iz a shlos: me darf dem richtiken shlisel.
A heart is a lock: you need the right key to it.

39

A hartz iz a shlos, ober a shlos efent men oich mit a noch-gemachten shlisel.
A heart is a lock, but a lock can be opened with a duplicated key.

40

A hunt iz a mol getrei'er fun a kind.
A dog is sometimes more faithful than a child.

41

A hunt on tsain iz ois hunt.
A dog without teeth is just not a dog.

42

A hunt on tsain varft zich oich oif a bain.
A dog without teeth also attacks a bone!

43

A katz meg oich kuken oifen kaisser.
A cat may also look at a king.

44

A katz vos m'yavket ken kain meiz nit chapen.
A meowing cat can't catch mice.

45

A kechin fardarbet zich nit.
A cook does not upset her own stomach.

46

A kind in shtub, ful in alleh vinkelech.
With a child in the house, all corners are full.

47

A kind vert geboren mit kulyaken un a man shtarbt mit ofeneh
hent.
A baby is born with clenched fists and a man dies with his
hands open.

48

A kind ken zein erger vi a gazlen, un men tantst noch oif zein
chasseneh.

A child may be worse than a robber, yet people (the parents) dance at his wedding.

49
A kindersher saichel iz oichet a saichel.
A child's wisdom is also wisdom.

50
A klaineh veibeleh ken oich hoben a groisseh moil.
A small woman can also have a big mouth.

51
A klap fargait, a vort bashtait.
A blow passes on, a spoken word lingers on.

52
A kloleh iz nit kain telegrameh: zi kumt nit on azoi gich.
A curse is not a telegram: it doesn't arrive so fast.

53
A kluger farshtait fun ain vort tsvai.
A wise man hears one word and understands two.

54
A kluger gait tsu fus un a nar fort in a kareteh.
A wise man walks on foot and a fool rides in a coach.

55
A kluger kop halt zich nit lang.
A smart head does not last long.

56
A kluger vaist vos er zogt, a nar zogt vos er vaist.
A wise man knows what he says, a fool says what he knows.

57
A lecherdiken zack ken men nit onfillen.
One can't fill a torn sack.

58
A ligen tor men nit zogen; dem emess iz men nit m'chuyev zogen.
A lie you must not tell; the truth you don't have to tell.

59
A ligner darf hoben a guten zechron.
A liar must have a good memory.

60
A ligner glaibt men nit, afileh az er zogt dem emess.
No one believes a liar even when he tells the truth.

61
A ligner hert zich zeineh ligen azoi lang ein biz er glaibt zich alain.
A liar tells his story so often that he gets to believe it himself.

62
A lustiger dales gait iber alles.
Happy poverty overcomes everything.

63

A maidel darf zich putsen far fremdeh bachurim un a veibel far'n aigenem man.

A maiden should pretty herself for strange bachelors and a young wife for her own husband.

64

A maidel iz vi samet—aderabeh, gib a glet!

A maiden is like velvet—come on, fondle her!

65

A makeh in yenem's orem iz nit shver tsu trogen.

Another man's disease is not hard to endure.

66

A mameh iz a dektuch (zi fardekt di chesroines fun di kinder).

A mother is like a veil (she hides the faults of her children).

67

A mentsh iz a mol shtarker fun eizen un a mol shvacher fun a flieg.

Man is sometimes stronger than iron and at other times weaker than a fly.

68

A melocheh iz a melucheh!

A craft is a kingdom!

69

A man, az er iz shener fun dem teivel, iz er shoin shain.
A man is handsome if he is only better looking than the devil.

70

A melocheh iz a melucheh, ober men hot nit kain minut menucheh.
A trade makes you a king but robs you of leisure.

71

A mentsh tracht un Got lacht.
Man thinks and God laughs.

72

A mentsh zol leben shoin nor fun neigerikeit vegen.
A man should stay alive if only out of curiosity.

73
A miesseh moid hot feint dem shpiegel.
A homely girl hates the mirror.

74
A mol iz der meshores mer yachsen vi der poretz.
Sometimes the servant is nobler than the master.

75
A mol iz der refueh erger fun der makeh.
Sometimes the remedy is worse than the disease.

76
A moshel iz nit kain rai'eh.
An example is no proof.

77
A nacht on shlof iz di gresteh shtrof.
A sleepless night is the worst punishment.

78
A nar bleibt a nar.
A fool remains a fool.

79
A nar darf hoben a sach shich.
A fool needs a lot of shoes.

80

A nar darf kain mosser nit hoben.
A fool needs no informer.

81

A nar farlirt un a kluger gefint.
A fool loses and a clever man finds.

82

A nar gait in bod arein un fargest zich dos ponim optsuvashen.
A fool goes to the baths and forgets to wash his face.

83

A nar gait tsvai mol dort, vu a kluger gait nit kain aintsik mol.
A fool makes two trips where a wise man makes none.

84

A nar git un a kluger nemt.
A fool gives and the clever one takes.

85

A nar ken a mol zogen a gleich vort.
Sometimes a fool can say something clever.

86

A nar ken fregen mer frages in a sho vi a kluger ken entferen in a yor.
A fool can ask more questions in an hour than a wise man can answer in a year.

87
A nar vakst on regen.
A fool grows without rain.

88
A nar vert nit elter un kalteh vasser vert nit kalyeh.
A fool doesn't age and cold water doesn't spoil.

89
A nei'er bezim kert gut.
A new broom sweeps clean.

90
A nemmer iz nit kain gibber.
A taker is not a giver.

91
A nevaireh kost oich gelt.
It costs money to sin.

92
A nogid a nar iz oich a har.
A foolish rich man is still a lord.

93
A nogid kumt op un an oreman kumt oif, iz noch nit gleich.
A rich man's fortune down and a poor man's fortune up—
they are still not even.

94
A noventer groshen iz besser vi a veiter kerbel.
A penny at hand is worth a dollar at a distance.

95
A patsh farhailt zich un a vort gedenkt zich.
A slap heals but a harsh word is remembered.

96
A pusten fas hilcht hecher.
An empty barrel reverberates loudly.

97
A sach mentshen zehen, nor vainik fun zai farshtai'en.
Many people see things but few understand them.

98
A shaineh froi iz a halbeh parnosseh.
A pretty wife is half a livelihood.

99
A shaineh maidel iz a karanteh shtikel s'choireh.
A pretty girl is the kind of goods that's always in demand.

100
A shain ponim kost gelt.
A pretty face costs money.

101

A shlecht veib iz noch tomid gerecht.

A shrewish wife can also be right.

102

A shlechteh mameh iz nitto.

There is no such thing as a bad mother.

103

A shlechteh sholem iz besser vi a guter krig.

A bad peace is better than a good war.

104

A shlimazel falt oifen ruken un tseklapt zich dem noz.

A fool falls on his back and bruises his nose.

105

A shlimazel kumt oich a mol tsu nutz.

Sometimes a piece of ill luck comes in handy.

106

A shloss iz gut nor far an orentlechen mentshen.

A lock is good only for an honest man.

107

A shpigel ken oich zein der grester farfirer.

A mirror can be the biggest deceiver.

108

A shtikel mazel iz vert merer vi a ton gold.
A little bit of luck is better than a ton of gold.

109

A shver hartz redt a sach.
A heavy heart talks a lot.

110

A shverer beitel macht a leicht gemit.
A heavy purse makes a light-hearted spirit.

111

A smagler regen iz gut far di felder un shlecht far di vegen.
A heavy rain is good for the fields and bad for the roads.

112

A toiber hot gehert, vi a shtumer hot dertsailt, az a blinder hot gezen, vi a krumer iz gelofen.
A deaf man heard how a mute told that a blind man saw a cripple run.

113

A toiten bevaint men ziben teg, a nar dem gantsen leben.
One mourns for the dead seven days, but for a fool a whole lifetime.

114

A tsaddik vos vais az er iz a tsaddik iz kain tsaddik nit.
A righteous man who knows he is righteous is not righteous.

115

A tserissen gemit iz shver tsum hailen.
A broken spirit is hard to heal.

116

A tsoreh kumt nit alain.
Trouble doesn't come alone.

117

A tsvaiteh veib iz vi a hiltserner fus.
A second wife is like a wooden leg.

118

A vaicher vort brecht a bain.
A gentle word can break a bone.

119

A veibeleh iz a teibeleh un a teiveleh.
A wife is a little dove and a little devil.

120

A vort iz azoi vi a feil—baideh hoben groisseh eil.
A word is like an arrow—both are in a hurry to strike.

121

A vort iz vert a sileh; shveigen iz vert tsvai.
Talk is worth a shilling; silence is worth two.

122
A veib a marsha'as iz a nega-tsora'as.
A shrewish wife is a scourge.

123
A yosem est a sach un a bitter hartz redt a sach.
An orphan eats too much, a bitter heart talks too much.

124
A yoven vert klug noch varmes.
A soldier becomes smart after eating some warm food.

125
A yung baimeleh baigt zich; an alter brecht zich.
A young tree bends; an old tree breaks.

126

A zaiger vos shtait iz besser vi a zaiger vos iz kalyeh; veil afileh
a zaiger vos shtait derveizt di richtikeh tseit tsvai mol a tog.

*A watch that has stopped is better than a watch that works
badly; for even a watch that has stopped shows the correct
time twice a day.*

127

Abi gezunt—dos leben ken men zich alain nemen.

Be sure to stay healthy—you can kill yourself later.

128

Aider azoi foren iz besser tsu fus gaien.

Better walk than ride like that.

129

Aider es kumt di nechomeh, ken oisgaien di neshomeh.

Things may get worse before they get better.

130

Aider gemain, besser alain.

Rather alone than with a lowly mate.

131

Aider me zogt arois s'vort, iz men a har; dernoch iz men a nar.

*Before you utter a word you are the master; afterwards you're
a fool.*

132

Ain foiler epel farfoilt di ander.
One rotten apple spoils the other.

133

Ain Got un azoi fil sonim.
One God and so many enemies.

134

Ain hartz fielt di andereh.
One heart feels another's affections.

135

Ain kind iz azoi vi ain oig.
Having an only child is like having one eye.

136

Ain man hot lib smetteneh un der anderer maftir.
One man likes sour cream and the other prayer.

137

Ain mol a saichel, dos tsvaiteh mol chain, dem dritten mol git
men in di tsain.
*The first time it's smart, the second time it's cute, the third
time you get a sock in the teeth.*

138

Ain nar iz a maivin oifen anderen.
One fool is an expert on the other.

139

Ain nar ken mer fregen aider tsen klugeh kenen entferen.
One fool can ask more than ten wise men can answer.

140

Ain nar macht a sach naronim.
One fool makes a lot of fools.

141

Ain tatteh tsen kinder derner; tsen kinder ain tatteh iz shver.
One father can support ten children; but it is difficult for ten children to support one father.

142

Aineh villen leben un kennen nit, un andereh kenen leben un villen nit.
Some want to live well and cannot, while others can live well and will not.

143

Ainem dacht zich az bei yenem lacht zich.
One always thinks that others are happy.

144

Ainem's mazel iz an anderen's shlimazel.
One's good luck is another's misfortune.

145

Ainer bovet un der anderer voint.
One builds the house and the other lives in it.

146

Ainer hakt holts un der anderer shreit: ei!
One chops the wood and the other shouts: oh!

147

Ainer iz a ligen, tsvai iz ligens, drei iz politik.
One lie is a lie, two are lies, but three is politics!

148

Ainer iz a maivin oif a p'shetel, der tsvaiter oif chazzer-hor,
ober alleh zeinen m'vinim oif a chazzen.
*One is an expert on scholarly discourse, another on bristles, but
all are experts on cantors.*

149

Ainer krigt far a k'nip a glet un a tsvaiter far a glet a patsh.
*One gets a caress for a pinch and the other for a caress gets
a slap!*

150

Ainer nait; der tsvaiter gait.
One sews the garment, the other wears it.

151

Ainer vaist nit dem anderens krenk.
One doesn't know another's sorrow.

152

Alain iz di neshomeh rain.
Don't depend upon others—do it yourself.

153
Alleh finger tuen gleich vai (alleh kinder zeinen gleich tei'er).
All fingers hurt alike (all children are equally dear to parents).

154
Allehs fleken ken men aroisnemen mit a bisseleh gold.
All spots can be removed with a little gold.

155
Alleh kalles zeinen shain; alleh maissim zeinen frum.
All brides are beautiful; all the dead are pious.

156
Alleh maissim hoben ain ponem.
All corpses have the same look.

157
Alleh meiles in ainem, iz nito bei kainem.
No one person possesses all the virtues.

158
Alleh shtumeh villen a sach reden.
All deaf-mutes have a great deal to say.

159
Alleh yiden kenen zein chazonim, ober maistens zeinen zai
haizerik.
Every Jew is a cantor, but he is hoarse most of the time.

160
Alleh shusters gaien borves.
All shoemakers go barefoot.

161
Alts drait zich arum broit un toit.
Everything revolves around bread and death.

162
Alts iz gut nor in der tseit.
Everything is good but only in its time.

163
Amol flegen di eltern lernen di kinder reden; heint lernen di kinder di eltern shveigen.
Once parents used to teach their children to talk; today children teach their parents to keep quiet.

164

An aizel derkent men bei di langeh oi'eren, a nar bei der langer tsung.

You can recognize a donkey by his long ears, a fool by his long tongue.

165

An alter freint iz besser vi a nei'eh tsvai.

One old friend is better than two new ones.

166

An iberik vort hot nit kain ort.

A superfluous word has no place.

167

An ofter gast falt tsu last.

A frequent guest becomes a burden.

168

An opgeshailteh ai falt oich nit alain in moil arein.

A peeled egg doesn't leap into the mouth by itself.

169

An oreman iz vi a lecherdiker zak.

A poor man is like a torn sack.

170

An oreman vil oich leben.

Even a poor man wants to live.

171
Arein iz di tir brait, un arois iz zi shmol.
The door to evil-doing is wide, but the return gate is narrow.

172
Aroif kletert men pavolyeh; arop kolert men zich shnell.
Uphill one climbs slowly; downhill one rolls fast.

173
Az a kluger redt tsu a nar, reden tsvai naronim.
When a wise man talks to a fool, two fools are talking.

174
Az a nar gait in mark, fraien zich di kremer.
When a fool goes shopping, the storekeepers rejoice.

175
Az a nar shveigt, vaist men nit tsi er iz a nar tsi a chochem.
When a fool keeps quiet, you can't tell whether he is foolish or smart.

176
Az a narishkeit gerot afileh amol, iz es fort a narishkeit.
When foolishness sometimes succeeds, it is still follishness.

177
Az alleh zuchen shaineh kalles, vu kumen ahin di miesseh maidlech?
If everybody looks for pretty brides, what's to become of the ugly girls?

178

Az a nar halt di ku bei di herner, ken zi a kluger melken.
If a fool holds the cow by the horns, a clever man can milk her.

179

Az an oreman macht chasseneh, krigt der hunt kadoches.
When a poor man makes a wedding, the dog gets the shivers!

180

Az der chossen iz der bagerter, darf di kalleh nit kain verter.
When the groom is desired, the bride doesn't need words.

181

Az der kluger failt, failt er veit!
When a clever man makes a mistake, does he make a mistake!

182

Az der kop iz a nar, ligt der gantser guf in der erd.
When the head is a fool, the whole body can go to hell.

183

Az der malamed kright zich mit der veib iz az och un vai tsu di talmidim.
When the teacher and his wife quarrel, the scholars get the worst of it.

184

Az der man iz tsu gut far der velt, iz er tsu shlecht far'n veib.
If a man is generally charitable, he will be unkind toward his wife.

185

Az der mogen iz laidik iz der moi'ech oich laidik.
When the stomach is empty, so is the brain.

186

Az der oirach hust, felt im a leffel.
When the guest coughs, he's lacking a spoon.

187

Az der oks falt, sharfen alleh di messer.
When the ox falls, everyone sharpens their knife.

188

Az der milner shlogt zich mitten koimen-kerer, vert der milner shvarts un der koimen-kerer veis.

When the miller fights with the chimneysweep, the miller becomes black and the chimneysweep white.

189

Az der soineh falt, tor men zich nit fraien, ober men haibt im nit oif.

When your enemy falls, don't rejoice; but don't pick him up either.

190

Az der talmid iz a voiler, iz der rebbi oich a voiler.

If the student is successful, the teacher gets the praise.

191

Az der tatteh shainkt dem zun, lachen baideh; az der zun shainkt dem tatten, vainen baideh.
When the father gives to his son, both laugh; but when the son gives to his father, both cry.

192

Az der yeger ken nit shissen, bleibt oich der hunt on a bissen.
If the hunter can't shoot, even his hound is left without a bite.

193

Az di balabosteh iz a shtinkerin, iz di katz a fresserin.
When the housewife is a slattern, the cat is a glutton.

194

Az di balabosteh iz brait, bakt zi braiteh broit.
If the housewife is stout, the loaves she bakes are large.

195

Az di hatslocheh shpilt, gilt ersht di chochmeh.
If luck plays along, cleverness succeeds.

196

Az di kalleh ken nit tantsen, zogt zi az di klezmorim kennen nit shpilen.
If the bride can't dance, she finds fault with the musicians.

197

Az di muter shreit oifen kind: "mamzer," meg men ir gloiben.

When a mother shouts at her child: "Bastard," you can believe her.

198

Az di velt zogt, zol men gloiben.

If everybody says so, there's some truth to it.

199

Az di vort iz in moil, iz men a har; az me lozt zi arois, iz men a nar.

While the word is still in your mouth, you are a lord; once you utter it, you are a fool.

200

Az dos hartz iz ful, gai'en di oigen iber.

When the heart is full, the eyes overflow.

201

Az dos mazel gait, kelbt zich der oks.

With luck, even your ox will calve.

202

Az drei zogen meshugeh, darf der ferter zogen, "Bim bom."

The majority rules.

203

Az du gaist oifen laiter, tsail di treplech.

When you climb a ladder, count the rungs.

204

Az du krigst zich, krig zich azoi du zolst zich kennen iberbeten.
In a quarrel, leave the door open for a reconciliation.

205

Az du kukst oif hoicheh zachen, halt tsu di hittel.
If you look up to high things, hold on to your hat.

206

Az du vest foren pamelech, vest du shneller onkumen.
If you drive slowly, you'll arrive more quickly.

207

Az es bashert ainem dertrunken tsu verren, vert er dertrunken
in a leffel vasser.
If one is fated to drown, he will drown in a spoonful of water.

208

Az es klingt, iz misstomeh chogeh.
When people talk about something, it is probably true.

209

Az es kumt der basherter, vert es in tsvai verter.
The right mate comes with the first date.

210

Az es kumt tsonvaitik fargest men kopvaitik.
When a toothache comes, you forget your headache.

211
Az es reg'nt mit gold, shtait der oreman untern dach.
When there's a shower of gold, the poor man stays under the roof.

212
A regen treibt arein in shtub un a baizeh veib treibt arois fun shtub.
Rain chases you into the house and a quarrelsome wife chases you out.

213
Az es vert geboren a maidel, iz a hatslocheh in der mishpocheh.
When a girl is born, it's a good omen for the family.

214
Az es vert nit besser, vert memaileh erger.
If it doesn't get better, depend on it, it will get worse.

215
Az es volt geven vainiker chazairim, volt geven vainiker mamzairim.
If there were fewer swine, there would be fewer bastards.

216
Az es zeinen nito kain andereh meiles, iz a zumer-shprinkeleh oich a meileh.
If a girl has no other virtues, even a freckle can be considered one.

217

Az Got git broit, giben mentshen puter.
When God gives bread, men give butter.

218

Az Got vil ainem dos hartz opshtoissen, git er im a groissen saichel.
When God wants to break a man's heart, he gives him a lot of sense.

219

Az Got vil, shist a bezim.
If God wills it, even a broom can shoot.

220

Az Got vil nit geben, ken men zich alain nit nemen.
If God does not give, one cannot take.

221

Az Got volt gelebt oif der erd, volt men im alleh fenster oisgeshlogen.
If God lived on earth, all his windows would be broken.

222

Az ich vel zein vi yener, ver vet zein vi ich?
If I would be like someone else, who will be like me?

223

Az in dem kufert ligt samet un zeid, ken men in trantes aroisgain far leit.

If velvet and silk are stored in the chest, one may appear among people in rags.

224
Az in droissen iz a vint, flit dos mist hoich.
When there is wind outside, the garbage flies high.

225
Az me chapt a patsh, bakumt men noch a soineh dertsu.
If one gets a slap in the face, one acquires an enemy as a bonus.

226
Az me est chazzer, zol rinnen fun bord.
If you're going to do something wrong, enjoy it!

227
Az me est nit kain k'nobel, shtinkt men nit.
If you don't eat garlic, you won't smell bad.

228
Az me handelt mit a nodel, gevint men a nodel.
If you invest a needle, you'll realize a needle.

229
Az me est op dem baigel, bleibt in kesheneh di loch.
If you eat your bagel, you'll have nothing in your pocket but the hole.

230

Az me est Shabbes kugel, iz men di gantseh voch zat.
If you eat pudding on the Sabbath, you'll be full all week.

231

Az me fregt a sheileh, vert traif.
If you ask the Rabbi a question, he will surely find something wrong.

232

Az me fregt, blonzhet men nisht.
If one asks, one does not err.

233

Az me gait tsevishen leiten, vaist men vos se tut zich in der haim.
When you go to your neighbors, you find out what is happening at home.

234

Az me ganvet avek dem ferd, farshliest men ersht di shtal.
After the horse has been stolen, the stable door is locked.

235

Az me gait gleich, falt men nit.
If you walk straight, you will not stumble.

236

Az me git, nem; az me nemt, shrei: "Gevalt!"
If you are given something, take it; if some one tries to take from you, cry "Help!"

237

Az me git ois a tochter, iz arop a horb fun der plaitseh.

When you marry off a daughter, a hump is off your back.

238

Az me grubt a grub far yenem, falt men alain arein.

If you dig a pit for someone else, you fall in it yourself.

239

Az me hot nit in kop, hot men in di fis.

If one hasn't got it in his head, he has it in his legs.

240

Az me hot nit tsu entfern, muz men farshveigen.

If one has nothing to answer, it is best to shut up.

241

Az me iz foil, hot men nit in moil.

The lazy person acquires no food.

242

Az me ken nit ariber, gait men arunter.

If you can't go over, go under.

243

Az me hot a sach tsu tun, laigt men zich shlofen.

If you have a lot to do, go to sleep.

244

Az me hot gelt, iz men klug un shain un men ken gut zingen.
If you have money, you are wise and good-looking and can sing well too.

245

Az me ken nit vi me vil, tut men vi me ken.
If you can't do as you wish, do as you can.

246

Az me klingt, iz oder a chsogeh oder a paiger.
When bells toll, it's either a holiday or a funeral for Gentiles.

247

Az me kumt iber di planken, bakumt men andereh gedanken.
If you cross over the fence, you acquire other ideas.

248

Az me kumt noch yerusheh, muz men oft batsolen k'vureh gelt.
If you come for the legacy, you often have to pay for the funeral.

249

Az me kumt traisten a yungeh almoneh, kvapet men zich nit tsu fardinen a mitsveh.
When one comes to comfort a young widow, he does not mean to perform a good deed.

250

Az me laight arein kadoches, nemt men arois a krenk.
If you invest in a fever, you will realize a disease.

251

Az me laigt arein, nemt men arois.
If you put something in, you can take something out.

252

Az me laigt zich nit gegessen, tsailt men di stolovanyes.
If you go to sleep with an empty stomach, you will count the beams on the ceiling.

253

Az me lebt mit a teivel, vert men a teivel.
He who lives with a devil, becomes a devil.

254

Az me ligt oif der erd, ken men nit fallen.
If you lie on the ground, you cannot fall.

255

Az me muz, ken men.
When one must, one can.

256

Az me redt a sach, redt men fun zich.
If you talk a lot, you talk of yourself.

257

Az me redt, derredt men zich.
If you keep on talking, you will end up saying what you didn't intend to say.

258
Az me lozt a chazzer aruf af'n bank, vil er af'n tish.
Give a pig a chair, he'll want to get on the table.

259
Az me redt a sach, ken men zich oisreden a narishkeit.
When one talks too much, one talks foolishness.

260
Az me redt zich arop fun hartsen, vert gringer.
When one pours out his heart, he feels lighter.

261
Az me shikt a nar oifen mark, frai'en zich di kremers.
When you send a fool to the market, the merchants rejoice.

262

Az me shloft mit hint shtait men oif mit flai.
If you lie down with the dogs, you get up with the fleas.

263

Az me shlogt di veib mit a kulteveh, vert derfun di gret nit veis.
Beating your wife with a paddle does not make the linen white.

264

Az me shmirt, fort men.
When you grease the palm, everything goes easy.

265

Az me shport nit dem groshen, hot men nit dem rubel.
If you don't save the penny, you'll not have the dollar.

266

Az me shveigt iz men a halber nar; az me redt iz men a gantser
nar.
*He who keeps quiet is half a fool; he who talks is a complete
fool.*

267

Az me tantst oif alleh chassenes, vaint men noch alleh maissim.
If you dance at every wedding, you'll weep at every funeral.

268

Az me trinkt alleh mol esik, vais men nit az es iz do a zisereh
zach.
*When one always drinks vinegar, he doesn't know that anything
sweeter exists.*

269

Az me tut zich loden, kumt men sei vi nit tsum shoden.
From litigation you can never recover your loss.

270

Az me vaint zich ois, vert gringer af'n hartz.
After a good cry, your heart is lighter.

271

Az me varft dem sod arein in yam, varft im der yam arois.
If you cast your secret into the sea, the sea will cast it out.

272

Az me vil a hunt a zets geben, gefint men a shteken.
When you want to beat a dog, be sure to find a stick.

273

Az me vil nit alt verren, zol men zich yungerhait oifhengen.
If you want to avoid old age, hang yourself in youth.

274

Az me zait gelt, vaksen naronim.
When you sow money, you reap fools.

275

Az me zetst arein a gandz in hober, shtarbt zi fun hunger.
Let a goose loose in oats and she will starve to death.

276

Az me zingt aider me shtait uf, vet men vainen aider me gait shlofen.

> *Sing before seven, cry before eleven.*

277

Az me zogt meshugeh, zol men gloiben.

> *When people say someone is crazy, believe it.*

278

Az me zucht, gefint men.

> *If you seek, you will find.*

279

Az men antloift fun fei'er, bagegent men dos vasser.

> *When you flee from fire, you run into water.*

280

Az men baizert zich op, gait op der ka'as.

> *When you give vent to your feelings, your anger leaves you.*

281

Az men chazert tsu fil iber vi gerecht men iz, vert men umgerecht.

> *If you repeat often enough that you're right, you will discover you're wrong.*

282

Az men dermont zich on dem toit, iz men nit zicher miten leben.

If you start thinking of death, you are no longer sure of life.

283

Az men falt bei zich, falt men oich bei andereh.

If you lose your self-respect, you also lose the respect of others.

284

Az men ganvet a sach ai'er, ken men oich verren a nogid.

If one steals a lot of eggs, one can also become rich.

285

Az men hot a gilderneh hentel, hot men dem leberel fun entel.

With golden hands, one can always afford the choicest delicacies.

286

Az men hot a shaineh veib iz men a shlechter chaver.

When you have a pretty wife, you are a bad friend.

287

Az men hot an ainikel, hot men tsvai kinder.

When you have a grandchild, you have two children.

288

Az men hot di matbai'eh, hot men di dai'eh.

If you have the money, you have the "say"!

289

Az men hot nit kain klinger, bleibt men ainer alain vi a finger.

If you have no dough, you are alone as a finger.

290

Az men iz a meister, iz ful der teister.

If you are a craftsman, your wallet is full.

291

Az men iz biz tsvantsik yor a kind, iz men tsu ain-un-tsvantsik a behaimeh.

If you're a child at twenty, you're an ass at twenty-one.

292

Az men ken nit beissen, zol men nit veizen di tsain.

Those who can't bite should not show their teeth.

293

Az men ken nit iberhar'n dos shlechteh, ken men dos guteh nit derleben.

If you can't endure the bad, you'll not live to witness the good.

294

Az men krigt zich miten rov, muz men sholem zein miten shainker.

If you're at odds with your rabbi, make peace with your bartender.

295

Az men lebt, derlebt men zich alts.
If you live long enough, you will live to see everything.

296

Az men maint, genart men zich.
To assume is to be deceived.

297

Az men shert di shaf, tsitteren di lemmer.
When the sheep are shorn, the lambs tremble.

298

Az men zitst in der haim, tsereist men nit kain shtivel.
If you stay at home, you won't wear out your shoes.

299

Az meshiach vet kumen, vellen alleh krankeh oisgehailt verren;
nor a nar vet bleiben a nar.
*When the Messiah comes, all the sick will be healed; only a
fool will stay a fool.*

300

Az m'iz hungerik est men broit.
If you're hungry enough, you can eat dry bread.

301

Az nito kain klaineh, iz nito kain groisseh.
When there are no small ones, there are no big ones.

302
Az oif dem hartsen iz bitter, helft nit in moil kain tsuker.

If there's bitterness in the heart, sugar in the mouth won't make life sweeter.

303
Az s'a regenboigen, veizt Got dem simen, az er iz undz moichel.

When there's a rainbow, it's a sign that God has forgiven our sins.

304
Az se brent, iz a fei'er.

Where there's smoke, there's fire.

305
Az se dunert in vinter iz der simen fun a zol.

Thunder in the winter is a sign of coming plenty.

306
Az s'iz in droissen a bloteh, frai'en zich di shusters.

When the streets are muddy, the cobblers rejoice.

307
Az s'iz nito in top, iz nito in teller.

If there's nothing in the pot, there's nothing on the plate.

308
Az tsvai zogen as du bist shikker, darf men zich laigen shlofen.

When two say you're drunk, it's best to go to sleep.

309

Azoi gait af der velt; ainer hot di beitel, der tsvaiter hot di gelt!
So it goes in this world: one has the purse, the other has the money.

310

Bainer on flaish iz do; flaish on bainer iz nito.
Bones without meat is possible; meat without bones is not possible.

311

Barat zich mit vemen du vilst; un tu miten aigenem saichel.
Ask advice from everyone, but act with your own mind.

312

Bei a shveren vogen iz gring tsu gain tsu fus.
Alongside a heavy wagon, it's easy to walk.

313

Bei nacht hert zich veit.
Prayer is heard best at night.

314

Beim glezel gefint men a sach guteh freint.
Over a glass of wine, you find many good friends.

315

Bei sholem—bayis iz men tsufriden mit a k'zayis.
When there is peace in the house, a bite suffices.

316

Beim oiskern di shtub gefint men alts.

When you sweep the house, you find everything.

317

Beitog tsum get, beinacht tsum bet.

By day they're ready to divorce, by night they're ready for bed.

318

Besser a gantser nar aider a halber chochem.

Better a complete fool than half wise.

319

Besser a guter soineh aider a shlechter freint.

Better a good enemy than a bad friend.

320

Besser a hon in hant aider an odler in himmel.

Better a hen in the hand than an eagle in the sky.

321

Besser a hunt in friden vi a zelner in krig.

Better a dog in peacetime than a soldier in war.

322

Besser a krummer fus aider a krumer kop.

Better a crooked foot than a crooked mind.

323
Besser a loit mazel aider a funt gold.
An ounce of luck is worth more than a pound of gold.

324
Besser a miesseh lateh aider a shaineh loch.
Better to have an ugly patch than a beautiful hole.

325
Besser a reicher shochen aider an oremer balabos.
Better a rich tenant than a poor landlord.

326
Besser a vaitik in hartz aider a charpeh in ponem.
Better a pain in your heart than shame before men.

327
Besser a yid mitun a bord, vi a bord mitun a yid.
Better a Jew without a beard than a beard without a Jew.

328
Besser ain alter freint vi a nei'eh tsvai.
One old friend is better than two new ones.

329
Besser ain freint mit gekechts aider hundert mit a krechtz.
Better one friend with a dish of food than a hundred with a sigh.

330

Besser ain ku in shtal aider tsen in feld.

Better one cow in the stable than ten in the field.

331

Besser alter vein aider alter koiches.

Better old wine than old strength.

332

Besser der soineh zol bei mir guts zen aider ich bei im shlechts.

Better that my enemy should see good in me than I should see evil in him.

333

Besser di t'no'im tsereissen aider di ketubeh.

Better to break off an engagement than a marriage.

334

Besser dos shlechteh fun guten aider dos guteh fun shlechten.

Better a bad deed of a good person than a good deed of a bad one.

335

Besser gornisht tsu machen aider tsu machen gornisht.

Better to do nothing than to make something into nothing.

336

Besser dos kind zol vainen aider der foter.

Better the child should cry than the father.

337

Besser fri'er bevorent aider shpeter bevaint.
Better caution at first than tears afterwards.

338

Besser fun a gratsh a patsh aider fun a nar a kush.
Better a blow from a wise man than a kiss from a fool.

339

Besser gut un a bissel aider shlechts un a fuleh shissel.
Better good and a little rather than bad and a lot of it.

340

Besser heint an ai aider morgen an ox.
Better an egg today than an ox tomorrow.

341

Besser herren kloles aider herren nebech.
Better to hear curses than to be pitied.

342

Besser mit a klugen in gehenem aider mit a nar in ganaiden.
It's better to be with a wise man in hell than with a fool in paradise.

343

Besser oif der velt nit tsu leben aider onkumen tsu a kind.
It is better not to live than to be dependent on children.

344
Besser tsu shtarben shtai'endik aider tsu leben oif di k'ni.
Better to die upright than to live on your knees.

345
Besser zich tsu vintshen aider yenem tsu shelten.
Better to pray for yourself than to curse another.

346
Bistu erlech mit dein veib, hostu a gezunteh leib.
If you're faithful to your wife, you'll have a healthy body.

347
Bitochen tsit tsum himmel, koved tsit tsu der erd.
Trust draws to heaven, honor to earth.

348
Biz zibetsik yor lernt men saichel un men shtarbt a nar.
Up to seventy years of age we learn wisdom and then we die fools.

349
Blut iz dicker fun vasser.
Blood is thicker than water.

350
Borgen macht zorgen.
Borrow causes sorrow.

351

Brecht zich a ring, tsefalt di gantseh kait.
One link snaps and the whole chain falls apart.

352

Bris, bar mitsveh, chasseneh, k'vureh-gelt—bald nossenen!
*Circumcision, confirmation, wedding, burial fee—all too soon
to be paid!*

353

Chain gait iber shain.
Charm is better than beauty.

354

Chasseneh gehat oif gich un geblibben in shtich.
Married in a hurry and stuck for good!

355

Chavershaft iz shtarker vi brudershaft.
Friendship is stronger than kinship.

356

Chutspeh gilt!
Nerve succeeds!

357

Darf men honig ven tsuker iz zis?
Who needs honey when sugar is sweet?

358

Dem bitersten mazel ken men farshtellen mit a shmaichel.
The bitterest misfortune can be covered up with a smile.

359

Dem ligner gloibt men afileh an emess oich nit.
The liar is not believed even when he tells the truth.

360

Dem oreman's yaitzer-horeh iz a skorinkeh broit.
The poor man's temptation is a loaf of bread.

361

Dem rosheh gait oif der velt, dem tsaddik oif yener velt.
The wicked fare well in this world; the saints in the life to come.

362

Dem rov's tochter tor nit vos dem beder's tochter meg.
The Rabbi's daughter is forbidden what the bath-house keeper's daughter is allowed.

363

Der barimer bleibt shteken in bloteh.
The boaster gets stuck in the mud.

364

Der bester ferd darf hoben a beitsh, der klugster man an aitseh un di frumsteh nekaiveh a man.
The best horse needs a whip, the wisest man advice and the chastest woman a man.

365

Der bester ferd iz nor a padleh ven er paigert.
The best horse is just a carcass when it dies.

366

Der cholem iz a nar un der shlof iz der har.
The dream is a fool and sleep's the master.

367

Der dales farshtelt di chochmeh.
Poverty hides wisdom.

368

Der dales hot a grobeh kop.
Poverty has a thick head.

369

Der dales laigt zich tsum ershten oifen ponem.
Poverty reveals itself first on the face.

370

Der derech hayosher iz alleh mol kosher.
The just path is always the right one.

371

Der doktor hot a refueh tsu altz, oder nit tsu dales.
The doctor has a remedy for everything but poverty.

372
Der emess hot alleh meiles, ober er iz a shemevdiker.
The truth has charm but it's shy.

373
Der emess iz a kricher.
Truth is a slowpoke.

374
Der emess iz der bester ligen.
Truth is the safest lie.

375
Der emess iz in di oigen, der ligen iz hinter di oigen.
The truth is in sight; the lie is behind the eyes.

376
Der emess ken arumgain a naketer, dem sheker darf men baklaiden.
The truth may walk around naked; the lie has to be clothed.

377
Der emess kumt arois azoi vi boimel oif der vasser.
The truth surfaces like oil on water.

378
Der emess lebt nit, der emess shtarbt nit, der emess matert zich!
The truth is not alive, the truth is not dead, it struggles!

379

Der emess shtarbt nit ober er lebt vi an oreman.
The truth doesn't die but it lives like a poor man.

380

Der ershter broigez iz der bester broigez.
The first quarrel is the best quarrel.

381

Der ganev hot a gringer melocheh un shlechteh chaloimes.
The thief has an easy job and bad dreams.

382

Der gehenem iz nit azoi shlecht vi dos kumen tsi im.
Hell is not so bad as the way to it.

383

Der grester rachmones iz oif an oremeh moid vos ligt in kimpet.
The most to be pitied is a poor maiden in childbirth.

384

Der grester shvimmer kon zich trenken.
Even the best swimmer can drown.

385

Der gleichster veg iz ful mit shtainer.
The smoothest way is full of stones.

386

Der guf iz a shvom, di neshomeh a t'hom.
The body is a sponge, the soul an abyss.

387

Der gvir hot dem saichel in teister.
The rich man has his brains in his billfold.

388

Der 'Innu-hadin iz erger vi der din alain.
Suspense is worse than the ordeal itself.

389

Der iz klug vos zein mazel gait im noch.
Who is smart? He whose fortune follows him.

390

Der ka'as un der tsoren farkirtzen di yoren.
Bad temper and anger shorten the years.

391

Der kluger bahalt dem saichel; der nar veist zein narishkeit.
A wise man conceals his intelligence; the fool displays his foolishness.

392

Der klugster mentsh benart zich.
The wisest man is guilty of folly.

393

Der koved iz fun dem vos git im, un nit fun dem vos krigt im.
Honor is measured by him who gives it, not by him who receives it.

394

Der leben iz di gresteh metsi'eh—me wrigt es umzist.
Life is the biggest bargain—we get it for nothing.

395

Der mazel macht klug, veil der mazel macht reich.
Fortune makes you smart, because fortune makes you rich.

396

Der mentsh fort un Got halt di laitses.
Man rides, but God holds the reins.

397

Der mentsh hot tsvai oigen, tsvai oiren, ober nor ain moil.
Man has two eyes, two ears, but only one mouth.

398

Der mentsh iz tsum shtarben geboren.
Man is born to die.

399

Der mentsh iz vos er iz, ober nit vos er iz geven.
Man is what he is, but not what he used to be.

400

Der mentsh tracht, un Got lacht.
Man thinks and God laughs.

401

Der mentsh tut hofen biz er vert antshlofen.
Man keeps hoping till he goes to his eternal slumber.

402

Der miesteh leben iz besser fun shensten toit.
The ugliest life is better than the nicest death.

403

Der mogen halt besser a sod vi di hartz.
The stomach keeps a secret better than the heart.

404

Der oilem iz a goilem.
The masses are asses.

405

Der oisher hot nit kain yoisher.
The rich have no sense of justice.

406

Der oks vais nit fun zein gevureh.
The ox is not aware of its strength.

407

Der oreman hot vainik feint, der reicher hot vainiker freint.
*The poor man's enemies are few, the rich man's friends are
even fewer.*

408

Der oreman tracht, der nogid lacht.
The poor think, the rich laugh.

409

Der ponem zogt ois dem sod.
The face tells the secret.

410

Der poretz iz gut un in hant iz di rut.
The master is kind but his hand holds the cane.

411

Der reicher est dos flaish un der oreman di bainer
The rich eat the meat; the poor the bones.

412

Der remez shlogt shtarker vi der emess.
A hint hits harder than the truth.

413

Der saichel fort oif oksen.
Wisdom travels by oxen.

414

Der saichel kumt noch di yoren.

Wisdom comes with the years.

415

Der shainker hot lib dem shikker, ober di tochter vet er im nit geben.

The saloonkeeper loves the drunkard, but he wouldn't give him his daughter in marriage.

416

Der shlof iz a ganev.

Sleep is a thief.

417

Der shlof iz der bester dokter.

Sleep is the best doctor.

418

Der shuster beim kapul un der top iz ful.

If the cobbler sticks to his last, his pot is full.

419

Der shuster redt fun der kapoteh; der backer fun der lopeteh.

The shoemaker speaks of his last and the sailor of his mast.

420

Der shversteh ol iz a laidikeh kesheneh.

The heaviest burden is an empty pocket.

421
Der shpigel nart kainem nisht op, nor dem miessen.
The mirror fools none but the ugly.

422
Der tsoren iz in hartsen a doren.
Anger is like a thorn in the heart.

423
Der veister veg iz der tsu der kesheneh.
The longest way is the one to the pocket.

424
Der vint flit avek un di kerpes bleiben.
The storm blows over but the driftwood remains.

425

Der volf hot nit moireh faren hunt, ober es gefelt im nit zein bilen.

The wolf is not afraid of the dog, but he hates his bark.

426

Der vos farshtait zein narishkeit iz a kluger.

He who is aware of his folly is wise.

427

Der vos gleicht tsu nemen, gleicht nit tsu geben.

He who likes to take does not like to give.

428

Der vos hot nit farzucht bittereh, vaist nit voz zies iz.

He who has not tasted the bitter does not understand the sweet.

429

Der vos shveigt maint oich epes.

He who is silent means something just the same.

430

Der vos zucht leichteh arbet gait zai'er mid tsu bet.

He who looks for light work goes very tired to bed.

431

Der yaitser-horeh shloft bei a maidel un iz oif bei a veibel.

Temptation in a maiden is asleep; in a wife it's awake.

432

Di alteh kei'en un di yungeh shpei'en.

What the old chew the young spit out.

433

Di boich farshlingt di kop miten saichel.

The stomach swallows up the head with the mind.

434

Di chasidem'lech zollen frailech zein, trinkt der rebenyu ois dem vein.

The rabbi drinks up the wine and orders his followers to be gay.

435

Der emess hot a sach ponimer.

The truth has many faces.

436

Di epeleh falt nit veit fun baimeleh.

The apple doesn't fall far from the tree.

437

Di ergsteh rechiles iz der emess.

The worst libel is the truth.

438

Di ershteh veib iz fun Got; di tsvaiteh iz fun mentshen.

Marriage with the first wife is made in Heaven; with the second, it's arranged by people.

439

Di ga'aveh ken fardarben, ober fun a ta'aveh vet men nit shtarben.

Haughtiness can do harm but you can't die from loving pleasure.

440

Di gantseh velt iz ful mit shaidim; treib zai chotsh fun zich arois.

The whole world is full of demons; you just exorcise them out of yourself.

441

Di gantseh velt iz nit meshugeh.

The whole world isn't crazy.

442

Di gantseh velt iz aim ganev.

The whole world is one thief.

443

Di gresteh narishkeit fun a nar iz vos er maint az er iz klug.

The biggest folly of the fool is that he thinks he is smart.

444

Di gresteh tsoreh—a veib a klafteh.

The biggest trouble—a shrewish wife.

445

Di grub iz shoin ofen un der mentsh tut noch hofen.

The grave is already dug and man still continues to hope.

446

Di hun hert dem hon's drosheh un zucht zich a kernd'l proseh.
The hen listens to the rooster's sermon and goes to look for a grain of corn.

447

Di kan fun blecher iz ful mit lecher.
The tinsmith's can is full of holes.

448

Di kats hot lib fish, nor zi vil di fis nit einnetsen.
The cat likes fish but she doesn't want to wet her paws.

449

Di klainer hartz nemt arum di groisseh velt.
The heart is small and embraces the whole wide world.

450

Di klensteh nekomeh farsamt di neshomeh.
The smallest vengeance poisons the soul.

451

Di klugeh gai'en tsu fus, un di naren foren.
Wise men go on foot and fools ride.

452

Di kro flit hoich un zetst zich oif a chazzer.
The crow flies high but settles on a hog.

453
Di libeh iz zis, nor zi iz gut mit broit.
Love is sweet, but it's nice to have bread with it.

454
Di lichtikeh velt iz fun shlimazel farshtelt.
The world is good, only bad luck casts a pall over it.

455
Di oi'eren heren nit vos dos moil redt.
The ears don't hear what the mouth utters.

456
Di oigen zollen nit zen, volten di hent nit genumen.
If the eyes wouldn't see, the hands wouldn't take.

457
Di pod-panes zeinen erger fun di panes alain.
Underlings are worse than masters.

458
Di roitsteh epel hot a vorm.
The reddest apple has a worm in it.

459
Di shich fun oreman's kind vaksen miten fisel.
The shoes of the poor man's kids grow with their feet.

460

Di shtileh vasserlech reissen ein di breges.
Quiet streams tear away the shores.

461

Di shversteh arbet iz arumtsugain laidik.
The hardest work is to go idle.

462

Di tefileh gait aroif un di brocheh gait arop.
The prayer ascends and the blessing descends.

463

Di varemsteh bet is di mames.
The warmest bed is mother's.

464

Di toireh hot kain grund nit.
The Scriptures have no bottom.

465

Di toireh leicht, di toireh brent, ober varemen varemt der
kerbel.
*The Torah gives light, the Torah burns, but only the dollar
gives warmth.*

466

Di toireh voint a mol in a churveh un biz'n haldz iz di purveh.
The Torah often dwells in a hovel, up to the neck in dirt.

467

Di toi'ern fun treren zeinen kain mol nit farshlossen.

The gates of tears are never shut.

468

Di tseit brengt vunden un hailt vunden.

Time brings wounds and heals them.

469

Di tseit iz der bester doktor.

Time is the best physician.

470

Di tseit ken alts ibermachen.

Time can alter everything.

471

Di tsung iz di feder fun hartsen.

The tongue is the pen of the heart.

472

Di vegen fun teshuveh zeinen nit vainiker farborgen vi di vegen fun zind.

The ways of repentance are as much hidden as the ways of sin.

473

Di veib oiket un der hunt kanoiket, dos kind chlipet, un der dales ripet.

The wife wails and the dog whimpers and the child whines and poverty howls!

474

Di velt hot feint dem massernik un dem mussernik.
The world hates the informer and the moralist.

475

Di velt iz a hekeleh: ainer darf tsum anderen.
The world consists of cogs: one depends on the other.

476

Di velt iz ful mit tsores, nor yederer fielt nor zeineh.
The world is full of troubles, but each man feels his own.

477

Di velt iz grois, ireh tsores noch gresser.
The world is big, its troubles still bigger.

478

Di velt zogt a vertel: besser mit a klugen farliren aider mit a nar gevinen.
The world has a saying: better to lose with a wise man than to win with a fool.

479

Di zun sheint lichtiker noch a regen.
The sun shines brighter after a shower.

480

Di zorgen laig op oif morgen.
Put off your worries for the morrow.

481

Dort vu men hot dich lib, gai vainik; vu men hot dich feint,
gai gor nit.

*Where people love you, go rarely; where you are hated, go
not at all.*

482

Dorten iz gut vu mir seinen nito.

That place seems good where we are not.

483

Dos besteh epel chapt ois der chazzer.

The pig snatches the best apple.

484

Dos gantseh leben iz a milchomeh.

All of life is a struggle.

485

Dos harts iz a halber novi.

The heart is something of a prophet.

486

Dos hindel vert miten shochet gevoint.

Fowls are inured to the killing.

487

Dos leben iz di gresteh metsi'eh—men krigt es umzist.

Life is the greatest bargain—you get it for nothing.

488

Dos leben iz nit mer vi a cholem, ober vek mich nit oif.
Life is no more than a dream, but don't wake me up!

489

Dos leben iz vi kinderhemdel—kurtz un bash.
Life is like a child's undershirt—short and soiled.

490

Dos mazel hot hazel.
Fortune provides shelter.

491

Dos oibershteh klaid fardekt di untershteh leid.
The outergarment conceals the inner torment.

492

Dos veremel nart op, un nit der fisher oder di vendkeh.
It's the bait that lures and not the fisherman or the tackle.

493

Drei zachen kon men nit bahalten: libeh, husten un dales.
Three things cannot be hidden: love, coughing and poverty.

494

Drei zachen vaksen ibernacht: revochim, diregelt un maiden.
Three things grow overnight: profits, rents and girls.

495

Durch shveigen ken men nit shteigen.
You can't get ahead with keeping quiet.

496

Durchlernen gantz shas iz a groisseh zach: durch lernen ain mideh iz a gressereh zach.
To learn the whole Talmud is a great accomplishment; to learn one good virtue is even greater.

497

Ehreh iz fil tei'erer far gelt.
Honor is much dearer than money.

498

Elteren kenen alts geben, nor kain mazel kenen zai nit geben.
Parents can provide everything except good luck.

499

Emess iz in sidder.
Truth one finds only in the prayerbook.

500

Emess iz nor bei Got un bei mir a bissel.
Truth is found only with God, and with me only a little.

501

Er glaibt nit in Got un bet zein genod.
He doesn't believe in God, yet asks His mercy.

502

Er hot avekgeganvet dem chumesh mit dem "loi sig-noiv."
He stole the Bible containing "Thou shalt not steal."

503

Er hot di vert fun a paim un far'reist di kop vi a baim.
He is worth a penny, yet he holds his head high like a tree.

504

Er hot dos leben fun Got un dos essen fun mentshen.
He owes his life to God and his living to men.

505

Er iz a seredniak—nit no'ent tsu a chochem un nit veit fun a nar.
He is mediocre—not near to a wise man, not far from a fool.

506

Er lebt mit der veib vi a brukiner mit a shtain.
He lives with his wife like a stonemason with a stone.

507

Er reit oif der kotshereh un zi reit oif dem fartach.
He rides the coach and she rides the apron.

508

Es iz a mitsveh a chazzer a hor arois tsu reissen.
It is a virtuous deed to pull a hair out of a pig.

509

Es iz besser a shandeh in ponem aider a vaitik in hartsen.
It is better to be embarrassed than heartbroken.

510

Es iz besser tsu leben in naches aider tsu shtarben in tsar.
It is better to live in joy than to die in sorrow.

511

Es iz bitter vi gal, un on gal ken men nit leben.
It's bitter like bile and without bile one cannot live.

512

Es iz bitter un shlecht ven der rabim iz umgerecht.
It's bitter and bad when the public is wrong.

513

Es iz groi di pai'eh un narish di dai'eh.
The temples are grey yet the mind is childish.

514

Es iz gut tsu fasten mit a polkeh fun a gandz un mit a pus-butelkeh.
Fasting is easy with a chicken leg and a half-bottle of wine.

515

Es iz gut tsu zein a gvir: der rov alain macht dem hesped.
It's good to be rich: the Rabbi himself makes the eulogy at your funeral.

516

Es iz leichter bei andereh chesroines tsu gefinen vi bei zich meiles.

It is easier to find faults in others than virtues in oneself.

517

Es iz nit azoi gut mit gelt vi es iz shlecht on dem.

It is not so good with money as it is bad without it.

518

Es iz nit azoi tei'er der geshank vi der gedank.

The gift is not as precious as the thought.

519

Es iz nit varem fun dobreh raideleh, nor fun dobreh maineleh.

Sweet talk doesn't make you warm but sweet meaning does.

520

Es iz shver tsu trogen, un avekvarfen tut bang.

It's too heavy to carry and too precious to throw away.

521

Es ken nit verren tsen ven ains iz nito.

You can't make ten when there isn't one to start with.

522

Es ken zein an erlecher shenker un a shefer a ganev.

There may be an honest saloon-keeper and a dishonest shepherd.

523
Es ken zein harb, oich di reichsteh arb.
The richest inheritance might become a burden.

524
Es kumen mekabel ponem zein dem oreman—a kalter vint un a baizeh hunt.
Who comes to greet a pauper? A cold wind and wild dogs.

525
Es lacht zich alain un es vaint zich alain.
One laughs alone and weeps alone.

526
Es libt zich alain, shemt zich alain.
He who praises himself will be humiliated.

527
Es shlogen zich aleh far di shtikeleh challeh.
All fight for a piece of bread.

528
Es shtait doch geshribben: chochmoh—shtikoh.
It is written: silence is wisdom.

529
Es shtumeh di tsinger ven du host in kesheneh klinger.
Evil tongues are silenced by the tinkle of coins in your pocket

530

Es stayet di bobben chasseneh tsu machen.
Great wealth will marry off even an old woman.

531

Es tut zich nit azoi gut vi es redt zich.
It isn't done as easily as it's said.

532

Es vais di katz vemes flaish zi hot oifgegessen!
The cat knows whose meat she ate!

533

Es bainer, vest du hoben a veissen chossen.
Chew on bones and you'll have a handsome husband.

534

Ess nit di lokshen far shabbes.
Don't eat the noodles before Sabbath.

535

Falen falt men alain, ober oiftsuhaiben zich darf men a hant
fun a freind.
*To fall down you manage alone but it takes friendly hands to
get up.*

536

Far a bissel libeh batsolt men miten gantsen leben.
For a little love you pay all your life.

537

Far a tsap hot men moireh fun forent, far a ferd fun hinten, far a nar fun alleh zeiten.

Every one fears a goat from in front, a horse from the rear and a fool on every side.

538

Far an akshen iz kain refueh nito.

For the disease of stubborness there is no cure.

539

Far der klenster toiveh vert men a ba'al-choiv.

For the smallest favor you become a debtor.

540

Far der teliyeh hoben mentshen mer moireh vi far Got alain.

Men fear the gallows more than God himself.

541

Far der velt muz men yoitseh zein vi far Got alain.

It's more important to please people than to please God.

542

Far gelt bakumt men alts, nor kain saichel nit.

Money buys everything except brains.

543

Far Got hot men moireh; far mentshen muz men zich hiten.

Fear God, but be wary of men.

544

Far kinder tsereist men a velt.
For your children's sake you would tear the world apart.

545

Far mein tir vet oich a mol zein a bloteh.
There may be mud before my door, too, some day.

546

Far morgen vet Got zorgen—un heint ver vet mir borgen?
Let God worry about the morrow—and for today, who will give me a loan?

547

Far umkoved antloif, ober yog zich nit noch koved.
Run away from an insult but don't chase after honor.

548

Far ziseh raidelech tsegai'en di maidelech.
Sweet talk makes the girls melt.

549

Faran dareh gvirim un feteh oremeleit.
Rich men are often lean and poor men fat.

550

Faren doktor un faren beder zeinen nito kain soides.
From a doctor and from a bathhouse-attendant, there are no secrets.

551

Farloreneh yoren iz erger vi farloreneh gelt.
Lost years are worse than lost dollars.

552

Farvos feift der dales? Veil er hot nor a dudeh!
Why does poverty whistle? Because it has nothing but a pipe!

553

Farvos klapt der dales? Veil er gait in klumpes!
Why does poverty knock? Because it walks in wooden shoes!

554

Fun a nar hot men tsar.
From a fool you have trouble.

555

Fun a vort vert a kwort.
One cross word brings on a quarrel.

556

Fun ain oks tsit men kain tsvai fellen nit arop.
From one ox you can't skin two hides.

557

Fun ain tifeh grub hot men mer vasser vi fun tsen flacheh.
*From one deep ditch comes more water than from ten shallow
ones.*

558

Fun akshones vegen gait men amol fun ganaiden in gehenem arein.

Out of stubborness many a man goes from heaven to hell.

559

Fun an alteh moid vert a getrei'eh veib.

An old maid becomes a faithful wife.

560

Fun an ek fun a chazzer ken men nit machen a shtreimel.

You can't make a hat out of a pig's tail.

561

Fun blut vert kain vasser nisht.

Blood doesn't turn into water.

562

Fun dein moil in Got's oi'eren arein.

From your mouth into God's ears!

563

Fun dem ber in vald zol men dos fel nit farkoifen.

Don't sell the skin off the bear that's still in the forest.

564

Fun eilenish kumt kain guts nisht arois.

No good comes out of hurrying.

565
Fun glik tsum umglik iz a shpan; fun umglik tsum glik iz a shtik veg.
From fortune to misfortune is a short step; from misfortune to fortune is a long way.

566
Fun handlen in gas mit klaineh zachen ken men kain groisseh gliken nit machen.
From peddling small goods on the streets you don't make big fortunes.

567
Fun hunger shtarbt men nor in a hunger-yor.
You can die of hunger only in a year of famine.

568
Fun iberessen cholyet men mer vi fun nit deressen.
From overeating one suffers more than from not eating enough.

569
Fun itlechen hoiz trogt men epes arois.
If you mix around, you learn quite a bit.

570
Fun kin'ah vert sin'ah.
Envy breeds hate.

571
Fun krimeh shiduchim kumen arois gleicheh kinder.
From bad matches good children are also born.

572
Fun loiter hofenung ver ich noch meshugeh.
Stuff yourself with hope and you can go crazy.

573
Fun naches lebt men nit; fun tsores shtarbt men nit.
One is not kept alive by joy, nor does sorrow alone cause death.

574
Fun rachmones un fun pachdones ken men zich nit ois'hailen.
For compassion and for cowardice there is no remedy.

575
Fun rechiles un soides antloif vi fun shaidim.
From tale-bearing and secrets run as from ghosts.

576
Fun shikker and fun shenker shtinkt mit bronfen.
The drunkard and the bartender both smell of whisky.

577
Fun sholem vegen meg men afileh a ligen zogen (ober sholem
tor kain ligen nit zogen).
*For the sake of peace one may even lie (but the peace itself
should not be a lie).*

578
Fun tsar vert der bain dar.
Sorrow makes the bones grow thinner.

579

Fun veiten nart men leiten; fun der noent, zich alain.

From afar you fool others; nearby, only yourself.

580

Fun yener zeit planken hot men andereh gedanken.

On the other side of the fence, you have a change of heart.

581

Ga'aveh un a laidiker teister zeinen nit kain por.

Conceit and an empty purse are no companions.

582

Gadles ligt oifen mist.

Pride lies on the dungheap.

583

Gai farshtai a maidel: zi vart oif di chasseneh un vaint tsu di chupeh.

Go understand a girl: she looks forward to her wedding and weeps as she walks to the marriage ceremony.

584

Ganaiden un gehenem ken men baideh hoben oif der velt.

Heaven and hell can both be had in this world.

585

Ganveh nit un fast nit.

Rob not, repent not.

586

Ganvet mein bruder, hengt men dem ganev.
If my brother steals, it is the thief who is hanged.

587

Geborgter saichel toig nit.
Borrowed brains have no value.

588

Gebroteneh teibelech fli'en nit in moil arein.
If you want something, you have to work for it!

589

Geganvet un opgegeben tsedokeh—haist geganvet.
Stealing and giving away for charity is still stealing.

590

Gehakteh leber iz besser vi gehakteh tsores.
Chopped liver is better than miserable troubles.

591

Gelebt vi a har un geshtorben vi a nar.
Lived like a lord and died like a fool.

592

Gelt brengt tsu ga'aveh un ga'aveh tsu zind.
Money causes conceit and conceit leads to sin.

593

Gelt farloren, gor nit farloren; mut farloren, alts farloren.

Money lost, nothing lost; courage lost, everything lost.

594

Gelt fiert di gantseh velt!

Money rules the world!

595

Gelt gait tsu gelt.

Money goes to money.

596

Gelt iz di besteh zaif vos nemt arois dem gresten flek.

Money is the best soap—it removes the biggest stain.

597

Gelt tsu fardinen iz gringer vi tsu halten.

It's easier to earn money than to keep it.

598

Gelteleh baleicht vi zun mein velteleh.

Money lights up my little world like the sun.

599

Geredt iz nit gebulen.

Talking isn't barking.

600
Gelt iz keilechdik—amol iz es do, amol iz es dort.
Money is round, it rolls away from you.

601
Geshmak iz der fish oif yenems tish.
Tasty is the fish from someone else's table.

602
Geshvindkeit iz nor gut floi tsu chapen.
Speed is only good for catching flies.

603
Gezunt kumt far parnosseh.
Health comes before making a livelihood.

604

Gleicher mit a haimishen ganev aider mit a fremden rov.
Rather with a hometown thief than a strange rabbi.

605

Glik on saichel iz a lecherdiker zak.
Luck without sense is a perforated sack.

606

Gold probirt men mit fei'er; a froi mit gold.
Gold is tested with fire; a woman with gold.

607

Gold sheint fun bloteh.
Gold glitters even in the mud.

608

Gornisht iz nisht shver—men badarf nor kenen.
Nothing is too difficult—you only have to know it.

609

Got alain iz nit reich—er nemt nor bei ainem un git dem
anderen.
*God is not rich; all He does is take from one and give to the
other.*

610

Got handelt nit un Got vandelt nit.
God does not bargain and God does not change.

611

Got helft dem oreman: er farhit im fun tei'ereh avaires.
God helps the poor man: He protects him from expensive sins.

612

Got hit op di naronim.
God watches over fools.

613

Got hot gegeben dem nar hent un fis un hot im gelozt loifen.
God gave the fool hands and feet and let him run.

614

Got hot lib dem oreman un helft dem nogid.
God loves the poor and helps the rich.

615

Got hot zich bashafen a velt mit klaineh veltelech.
God created a world full of many little worlds.

616

Got iz a foter; dos mazel iz a shtif-foter.
God is a father; luck is a stepfather.

617

Got nemt mit ain hant un git mit der andereh.
God takes with one hand, and gives with the other.

618
Got shikt di kelt noch di klaider.
God send the weather according to your needs.

619
Got shikt di refueh far der makeh.
God sends the remedy for the disease.

620
Got shtroft, der mentsh iz zich noikem.
God punishes but man takes revenge.

621
Got shtroft mit ain hant, un bentsht mit der anderen.
God punishes with one hand and blesses with the other.

622
Got zitst oiben un poret unter.
God sits on high and makes matches below.

623
Got zol hiten fun ain hemd, ain oig un ain kind.
God save us from having one shirt, one eye, and one child.

624
Got zol mich bentshen, ich zol nit broichen mentshen.
God should bless me so that I don't need people.

625

Gring iz tsu krigen a soineh; shver iz tsu krigen a freind.
It's easy to acquire an enemy; hard to acquire a friend.

626

Gring tsu zogen, shver tsu trogen.
Easy to promise, hard to fulfill.

627

Gringer iz herren a sod aider hiten a sod.
It is easier to hear a secret than to keep it.

628

Guteh p'sures hert men fun der veitens.
Good tidings are heard from far away.

629

Guteh freint fun veiten.
You are better friends at a distance.

630

Guteh tsolen, shlechteh monen.
The good ones pay, the bad ones demand.

631

Guts gedenkt men, shlechts filt men.
Kindness is remembered, meanness is felt.

632

Gutskeit iz besser fun frumkeit.

Kindness is better than piety.

633

Halten shabbes iz gringer vi machen shabbes.

To observe the Sabbath is easier than to make it.

634

Handelshaft iz kain brudershaft.

Don't mix business with pleasure.

635

Himmel un erd hoben geshvoren az kain zach zol nit zein
farloren.

Heaven and earth have sworn that the truth shall be disclosed.

636

Hint beissen zich iber a bain un availim iber a yerusheh.

Dogs fight over a bone and mourners over an inheritance.

637

Hiten zol men zich far di freind, nit far di feint.

Beware of your friends, not your enemies.

638

Hob lib dem tsvaiten un loz zich nit naren fun dem ershten.

*Love the other fellow and don't let yourself be fooled by the
first.*

639

Hob mich vainik lib nor hob mich lang lib.

Better love me little, but love me long.

640

Hob nit kain moireh ven du host nit kain ander braireh.

Don't be scared when you have no other choice.

641

Hof oif nissim un farloz zich nit oif a nes.

Hope for miracles but don't rely on one.

642

Hofen un haren machen klugeh far naren.

Hoping and waiting makes fools out of clever people.

643

Honik oifen tsung, gall oifen lung.

Honey on the tongue, gall in the heart.

644

Host broit mit puter, iz der mazel a guter.

If you have bread and butter, you have good luck.

645

Host du, halt; vaist du, shveig; kenst du, tu!

If you have, hold on to it; if you know, be silent; if you can, do!

646

Iber a tsvikel macht men kalyeh kain hemd.

One doesn't spoil a shirt because of one corner.

647

Ibergekumeneh tsores iz gut tsu dertsailen.

It's good to talk about troubles that are over.

648

In a guter sho tsu reden; in a baizer sho tsu shveigen.

In a lucky time it's good to talk; in an unlucky time, it's better to be silent.

649

In a shainem epel gefint men amol a vorem.

In a good apple you sometimes find a worm.

650

In bod zeinen alleh gleich.

At the baths all are equal.

651

In der yugent a behaimeh; oif der elter a ferd.

In youth a cow; in old age a horse.

652

In shissel ken nit zein mer vi in top.

You can't have more in the plate than you have in the pot.

653

In shlof zindikt nit der mentsh, nor zeineh chaloimes.
In sleep, man doesn't sin, but his dreams do.

654

In shpigel zet itlecher zein besten freind.
In the mirror everybody sees his best friend.

655

In toch iz yeder tsad gerecht.
In a quarrel, each side is right.

656

In yenems moil tsailt men nit di tsain.
You don't count the teeth in someone else's mouth.

657

Itlecheh bas-yechideh hot zich ir chaindel.
Every only daughter has her charms.

658

Itlecheh shtot hot ir meshugenem.
Every town has its fool.

659

Itlecher mentsh hot zich zein shigoyen.
Every man has a madness of his own.

660

Iz di shteig enger, hodeven zich di gendz besser.
When the coop is secure, the geese will grow fatter.

661

Iz do a braireh, darf nit zein kain moireh.
When there is a way out, there is no need for fear.

662

Kadeges klepen zich tsu klaider un krenk tsum guf.
Thistle sticks to clothes and disease to the body.

663

Kain braireh iz oich a braireh.
No choice is also a choice.

664

Kain naronim badarf men nisht tsu zai'en; zai vaksen alain.
Fools don't have to be sown; they grow up by themselves.

665

Kain umzister soineh iz nito; me batsolt far im.
There are no enemies for free; you have to pay for them.

666

Kainer bahalt nit; nit der rosheh zein rishes, nit der nar zein narishkeit.
No one hides—neither the wicked his wickedness nor the fool his folly.

667

Kainer hot nit kain legoteh tsu hoben charoteh.
Nobody has a monopoly on regret.

668

Kainer iz nit azoi toib vi der vos vil nit herren.
There's no one as deaf as he who will not listen.

669

Kainer vaist nit vemes morgen es vet zein.
No one knows what the morrow will bring.

670

Kainer vaist nit vemen der shuch drikt.
You never know the other fellow's troubles.

671

Kainer zogt nit "Oi" az se tut nit vai.
One doesn't cry "Ouch" if he's not in pain.

672

Kargeh leit dinen der avoideh-zoreh.
Misers are idol worshippers.

673

Kargen iz erger vi ganvenen.
To be miserly is worse than to steal.

674

Kenen toireh iz nit kain shter tsu avaireh.

Knowledge of the Torah is no deterrent to sin.

675

A kind's treren reissen himlen.

A child's tears reach the heavens.

676

Kinder brengen glik, kinder brengen umglik.

Children bring good fortune, children bring misfortune.

677

Kinder un gelt iz a shaineh velt.

Children and money make a nice world.

678

Kirtzer geshlofen, lenger gelebt.

The less you sleep, the more you get out of life.

679

Klaider bahalten dem mum.

Clothes conceal the blemish.

680

Klaider machen dem mentshen.

Clothes make the man.

681
Klaineh genaivim hengt men; groisseh shenkt men.
Petty thieves are hanged; big thieves are pardoned.

682
Klaineh kinder, klaineh fraiden; groisseh kinder, groisseh laiden.
Little children, little joys; bigger children, bigger sorrows.

683
Klaineh kinder lozen nit shlofen; groisseh kinder lozen nit ruen.
Small children don't let you sleep; big children don't let you rest.

684
Klaineh lozen nit kei'en; groisseh lozen nit banei'en.
Little ones don't let you chew; big ones don't let you buy anything new.

685
Klugheit iz besser fun frumkeit.
Wisdom is better than sanctimony.

686
Kolzman es rirt zich an aiver, klert men nit fun kaiver.
As long as one limb stirs, one does not think of the grave.

687
Kratsen un borgen iz nor gut oif a veil.
Scratching and borrowing is only good for a while.

688
Kreplach essen vert oich nimis.
One gets tired of eating only kreplach.

689
Krich nit tsu hoich, vestu nit darfen falen.
Don't climb too high and you won't have to fall.

690
Laig nit op oif morgen vos du kenst heint bazorgen.
Don't put off till tomorrow what you can do today.

691
Laig zich nit mit a gezunter kop in a kranken bet.
Don't lie down with a healthy head in a sick bed.

692
Leichteh libes, shvereh shodens.
Easy loves, heavy damages.

693
Lei'en darf men mit aides, geben zol men on aides.
*Lending should be done with witnesses; giving, without
witnesses.*

694
Libeh iz vi puter, s'iz gut mit broit.
Love is like butter, it's good with bread.

695

Libeh un hunger voinen nit in ainem.
Love and hunger don't dwell together.

696

Loif nit noch dem koved, vet er alain tsu dir kumen.
*Honors will come to you by themselves if you don't run after
them.*

697

Loshen horeh iz di ergsteh mideh un gresteh tsoreh.
Gossiping is the worst habit and the biggest calumny.

698

Loz zein an ergerer, abi an anderer.
Let it be worse, as long as it's a change.

699

Men farshpetikt nit chasseneh hoben un shtarben.
Marrying and dying are two things for which one is never late.

700

Man un veib zeinen ain leib.
Husband and wife are like one flesh.

701

Mazel un chain koift men nit in kremel.
Luck and charm cannot be purchased in a store.

702

Me darf nit zein shain, nor chainevdik.

You don't have to be pretty if you are charming.

703

Me ken dem barg mit a shpendel nit avektrogen.

A mountain cannot be moved with a splinter.

704

Me darf leben un lozen leben.

Live and let live.

705

Me ken dem yam mit a kendel nit ois'shepen.

The ocean cannot be emptied with a can.

706

Me ken nit foren oif alleh yariden oif ain mol.

You can't ride in all directions at one time.

707

Me ken nit iberloifen di levoneh.

You can't outrun the moon.

708

Me ken nit tantsen oif tsvai chassenes oif ain mol.

You can't dance at two weddings at the same time!

709

Me lernt zich biz zibetsik un shtarben shtarbt men a nar.

Man learns till seventy but still dies an ignoramus.

710

Me tor nit veizen a nar halbeh arbet.
You don't show a fool a job half-done.

711

Me zogt: a nar hot lib zieh zachen—dos hoben klugeh
oisgetracht.
*The saying that fools like sweets is an invention of smart
people.*

712

Me zol nit darfen onkumen tsu kinder.
Pray that you may not be a burden to your children.

713

Me zol nit gepruft verren tsu vos me ken gevoint verren.
*Pray that you may never have to endure all that you can learn
to bear.*

714

Melocheh bez deigeh.
To have a trade is to be free of worry.

715

Men bagrist noch di klaider, men baglait nochen saichel.
*When you enter you are greeted according to your dress; when
you leave, you are bade farewell according to your wisdom.*

716

Men iz dir moichel di t'shuveh, nor tu nit di avaireh.
Never mind the remorse, don't commit the sin.

717

Men ken handlen mit trantes un zich klaiden in samet.

You may deal in rags and dress in velvet.

718

Men ken machen dem cholem gresser vi di nacht.

You can make a dream bigger than the night.

719

Mer a chessorin, mer nadan.

More blemish, more dowry.

720

Miesseh maiden lozen zich raiden.

Homely girls let themselves be seduced.

721

Mit a barsht un a nodel bahalt men dem dales.

With a brush and a needle poverty can be covered up.

722

Mit a foilen shteken ken men nit aroistreiben dem dales.

With a lazy stick you cannot chase away want.

723

Mit a groissen roifeh gait a groisser malech.

A great doctor is accompanied by a great angel.

724

Mit a guten gast frait men zich ven er kumt arein; mit a
shlechten gast, ven er gait avek.

*With a good guest, you are happy when he arrives; with a bad
one, when he leaves.*

725

Mit a krechtz batsolt men nit a choiv.

You cannot pay a debt with a sigh.

726

Mit a meisseh un mit a ligen ken men nor kinder farvigen.

*With a fairy tale and with a lie you can lull only children
to sleep.*

727

Mit a nar tor men nit handlen.

With a fool you have no right to do business.

728

Mit a yid iz gut kugel essen, ober nit af ain teller.

It's good to eat pudding with a Jew, but not from one plate.

729

Mit ain hant shtroft Got un mit der anderer bentsht er.

With one hand God punishes and with the other he blesses.

730

A ligner glaibt kainmol nit.

A liar never believes anyone else.

731
A shveigendiker nar is a halber chochem.
A quiet fool is half a sage.

732
Bei nacht zeinen alleh ki shvartz.
At night all cows are black.

733
Nitzochen farshikert on vein.
Success intoxicates without wine.

734
Zingen ken ich nit, ober a maivin bin ich.
I can't sing, but I'm an expert on it.

735
Onkuken kost kain gelt.
It costs nothing to look.

736
Tachrichim mach men on keshenes.
Shrouds are made without pockets.

737
Ven di bobbeh volt gehat a bord, volt zi geven a zaideh.
If your grandmother had a beard, she'd be your grandfather.

738

Vos toig dir der chaner cholem, ven der frimorgen iz kalt?
What's the use of a beautiful dream, if the dawn is chilly?

739

Mit alleh meiles iz nito.
Nothing is perfect.

740

Mit di yoren verren shvacher di tsain un der zikoren.
As the years go by, the teeth and the memory grow weaker.

741

Mit emess kumt men far Got.
With truth man reaches God.

742

Mit fremdeh hent iz gut fei'er tsu sharren.
It's good to poke the fire with somebody else's hands.

743

Mit fremden saichel ken men nit leben.
With another's common sense one cannot live.

744

Mit geduld shept men ois a k'val.
With patience you can drain a brook.

745

Mit geduld boi'ert men durch afileh a kizelshtain.
With patience you can even bore through granite.

746

Mit gelt ken men alles.
Money can do everything.

747

Mit gelt tor men nit stolzieren, veil me ken es gleich farlieren.
Don't boast of your money because you can easily lose it.

748

Mit Got tor men zich nit shpilen. Ershtens, tor men nit, un tsvaitens, lozt er nit.
You don't play around with God! First, it's not allowed and second, He won't let you.

749

Mit honik ken men chapen mer fligen vi mit essik.
With honey you can catch more flies than with vinegar.

750

Mit ligen kumt men veit, ober nit tsurik.
With lies you will go far, but not back again.

751

Mit mazel ken men alles.
With luck, everything is possible.

752

Mit rugzeh fort men nit veit.
With anger you don't get too far.

753

Mit shnai ken men nit machen gomolkes.
You can't make cheesecakes out of snow.

754

Mit toireh vert men in ergets nit farfalen.
With knowledge you are nowhere lost.

755

Mit vos far an oig men kukt oif ainem, aza ponem hot er.
The way you look at a man so he appears to you.

756

Mit zabonges chapt men faigelech un mit matones—maidelech.
With nets you catch birds and with presents—girls.

757

Mit z'chus-oves batsolt men nit kain choives.
You cannot pay a debt with a noble pedigree.

758

Miten malach hamovess treibt men nit kain katovess.
You can't jest with the Angel of Death.

759

Naches fun kinder iz tei'erer fun gelt.
Pride in children is more precious than money.

760

Nadan kenen elteren geben, ober nit kain mazel.
Parents can give a dowry but not luck.

761

Naronim un kropeveh vaksen on regen.
Fools and weeds grow without rain.

762

Nein rabonim kenen kain minyen nit machen ober tsen shusters yoh.
Nine rabbis cannot make a quorum but ten shoemakers can.

763

Nisht azoi gich macht zich vi es tracht zich.
Things are not as quickly achieved as conceived.

764

Nisht alleh tsores kumen fun himmel.
Not all troubles come from heaven.

765

Nit als vos glanst iz gold.
All that glitters is not gold.

766

Nit der reicher tsolt; der erlecher tsolt.
Not the rich who pay; the honest pay.

767

Nit der shteken helft, nor der guter vort.
It's not the stick that helps but the kind word.

768

Nit dos iz shain vos iz shain, nor dos vos gefelt.
Not that which is beautiful but that which pleases is beautiful.

769

Nit far klugeh iz gelt, nit far shaineh iz klaider.
Not the wise have money, not the beautiful have (nice) clothes.

770

Nit fun a shaineh tsurkeh vert a guteh veib.
A pretty face doesn't make for a good wife.

771

Nit in z'chus-oves, nit in yerusheh—in zich zuch kedusheh.
Not in the merit of ancestors, nor in inheritance—in yourself you search for holiness.

772

Nit itlecher vos zitst oiben-on iz a pan.
Not all who sit at the head-table are aristocrats.

773

Nit kain entfer iz oich an entfer.
No answer is also an answer.

774
Nit kain groisser chochem, nit kain klainer nar.
He's no great sage and no small fool.

775
Nit mit shelten un nit mit lachen ken men di velt ibermachen.
Neither with curses nor with laughter can you change the world.

776
Nit af alleh mol shlecht, un nit af alleh mol gut.
Things can't be bad all the time, nor good all the time.

777
Nit yeden mesles treft zich a nes.
Miracles don't happen every day.

778
Nit yeder hartz vos lacht iz frailech.
Not every heart that laughs is really cheerful.

779
Nit yeder iz tsufriden mit zein ponem, ober mit zein saichel iz yeder tsufriden.
Not everybody is content with his looks, but everyone is content with his brains.

780
Nit yederer oif vemen hunt bilen iz a ganev.
Not everyone the dogs bark at is a thief.

781

Noch dem oreman shlept zich der shlimazel.
Bad fortune follows the poor man.

782

Noch di chupeh iz shpet di charoteh.
After the wedding it's too late to have regrets.

783

Nochen toit vert men choshev.
After death one becomes important.

784

Nor bei zein aigenem tish ken men zat verren.
Only at your own table can you be sated.

785

Nor in cholem zeinen meren vi beren.
Only in dreams are the carrots as big as bears.

786

Nor naronim farlozen zich oif nisim.
Only fools rely on miracles.

787

Noit brecht eizen.
Necessity breaks iron.

788

Oder es helft nit oder men darf es nit.
Either it doesn't help or it isn't needed.

789

Oder gor oder gornit.
All or nothing.

790

Oib der shuch past, kenst im trogen.
If the shoe fits, wear it.

791

Oib di velt vet verren oisgelaizt, iz es nor in z'chus fun kinder.
If the world will ever be redeemed, it will be only through the merit of children.

792

Oib zein vort volt gedint als brik, volt men moireh hoben aribergain.
Were his word a bridge, it would be risky to pass over it.

793

Oif a meisseh fregt men kain kasheh nit.
Don't ask questions about fairy tales.

794

Oif a mentshen iz nit kain rachmones; a rachmones iz oif nit a mentshen.
A man is not to be pitied; pitiable is one who is not a man.

795
Oif a fremder bord iz gut zich tsu lernen sheren.
It's good to learn to barber on someone else's beard.

796
Oif a nar iz kain kasheh nit tsu fregen un kain pshat nit tsu
zogen.
You should not ask a fool a question nor give him an ex-
planation.

797
Oif a nar tor men nit faribel hoben.
You must not take offense at anything a fool does.

798
Oif shainem iz gut tsu kuken; mit a klugen iz gut tsu leben.
It's good to behold beauty and to live with wisdom.

799

Oif a tserisseneh freintshaft ken men kain lateh nit laigen.
You can't patch up a torn friendship.

800

Oif a vund tor men kain zalts nit shiten.
You mustn't pour salt on a wound.

801

Oif aigeneh kinder iz yederer a blinder.
When it comes to one's own children, then everybody is blind.

802

Oif der shpitz tsung ligt di gantseh velt.
On the tip of the tongue, lies the fate of the entire world.

803

Oif der tir fun derfolg iz ongeshriben "shtup" un "tsi."
The door of success is marked "push" and "pull."

804

Oif fremder erd boit men nit.
One doesn't build on foreign ground.

805

Oif gelt shtait di velt.
The world stands on money.

806

Oif Got tor men kain kasheh nit fregen.
Trust in God.

807

Oif itlechen terets ken men gefinen a nei'eh kasheh.
To every answer you can find a new question.

808

Oif mist iz geroten korn.
Corn can grow on manure.

809

Oif morgen zol Got zorgen.
Let God worry about tomorrow.

810

Oif nisim tor men zich nit farlozen.
Don't depend on miracles.

811

Oif drei zachen shtait di velt: oif gelt, oif gelt, un oif gelt.
The world stands on three things: money, money, and money.

812

Oifen balken ken kain korn nit geroten.
You can't grow corn on the ceiling.

813
Oif tsedokeh iz oich do chazokeh.
Charity is also a habit.

814
Oif vemens vogen me zitst, zingt men dem lied.
People always sing the tune that pleases their host (or bene-factor).

815
Oif "volt ich" un "zolt ich," borgt men nit kain gelt.
No one lends money on "I could have" and "I should have."

816
Oif yenems simchah hot men a guten appetit.
At other people's parties one eats heartily.

817
Oif zeineh raid ken men nit boien kain binyen.
On his words no building could be built.

818
Oifen goniff brent dos hittel.
A guilty man is always self-conscious.

819
Oifen goniff in a tsilinder brent nit dos hittel.
A thief with connections is not self-conscious.

820

Oif nichteren mogen ken men kain zach nit fartrogen.
An empty stomach cannot tolerate anything.

821

Oisbrukirt mit tsores iz der veg tsum bais-hakvores.
The road to the cemetery is paved with suffering.

822

On gelt iz kain velt.
Without money, it is no world (to live in).

823

On a teretz iz gor kain derech-eretz.
Without an excuse there's no respect.

824

On a tsung iz vi on a glok.
Without a tongue is like without a bell.

825

On mazel toig gor nit.
Without luck, nothing will succeed.

826

On mo'es iz tomid a to'es.
Being without money is always a mistake.

827

Orem iz nit kain shandeh, abi nit shmarkateh.

Poverty is no disgrace, just so it isn't filthy.

828

Orem iz nit kain shand, ober oich kain groisser koved nit.

Poverty is no disgrace, but also no great honor.

829

Parnosseh iz a refueh tsu alleh krenk.

A good livelihood is a cure for all ills.

830

Patsh zich nit in beicheleh, ven fisheleh iz noch in teicheleh.

Don't rub your belly when the little fish is still in the pond.

831

Protsent fun kinder iz tei'erer vi protsent fun gelt.

Dividends from children is more precious than from money.

832

Purim iz kain yontev nit un kadoches iz nit kain krenk.

Purim is no holy day and fever is no disease.

833

Rachmones hot raineh kavones.

Pity has pure intentions.

834

Red besser vegen zich guts vider vegen dem andern shlechts.
It's better to praise yourself than to disparage others.

835

Reden iz gut, shveigen noch besser.
Speech is good, silence even better.

836

Reden iz shver un shveigen ken men nit.
Speech is difficult, but silence is impossible.

837

Reden iz zilber, shveigen iz gold.
Speech is silver, silence is golden.

838

Reboineh-shel-oilem, haib mich nit uf, varf mich nit arop.
Father in heaven, don't raise me up, don't cast me down.

839

Reboineh-shel-oilem: kuk arop fun dem himmel un kuk dir on
dein velt.
Father in heaven, look down from heaven and see your world.

840

Rov oder beder, alleh hoben soinem.
Whether a rabbi or a bath-house keeper, all have enemies.

841

Saichel iz an aideleh zach.

Wisdom is a precious thing.

842

Saichel krigt men nisht oif di berzeh.

Wisdom can't be purchased in the market.

843

Shabbes hot der rosheh in gehenem oich ru.

On the Sabbath even the wicked in hell have rest.

844

Shaineh shveigen iz shener vi shain reden.

Dignified silence is better than dignified speech.

845

Shlimazel, vohin gaist du? Tsum oreman!

Bad fortune, where goest thou? To the poor man!

846

Shpeiz kocht men in top un koved krigt der teller.

The food is cooked in a pot and the plate gets the honor.

847

Shpilt tsu di shoh, iz kain zind nito.

If done at the right time, it is not a sin.

848

Shpor, shpor; kumt der shvartz yor un nemt tsu gor!
Save, save; comes the evil year and takes it all away!

849

Shrei'en helft nit, ober a shteken helft.
Scolding won't help, but the stick would.

850

Shtarben un chasseneh hoben farshpetigt men nit.
It's never too late to die or get married.

851

Shtil vasser grobt tif.
Still waters run deep.

852

Shveigen haist geret.
Silence gives consent.

853

S'iz shlecht tsu essen fremden broit.
It's hard to eat a stranger's bread.

854

Tinken haist nit trinken.
Dipping isn't drinking.

855

Tint trikent shnell ois; treren nisht.

Ink dries quickly; tears don't.

856

Toireh iz di besteh s'choireh.

Knowledge of the Scriptures is the best wares.

857

Toireh kumt nit b'yerusheh.

Learning cannot be inherited.

858

Tsedokeh zol kain gelt nit kosten un g'milas-chassodim zolen kain agmas-nefesh nit farshafen, volten geven di velt fil tsadikim.

If one could do charity without money and favors without aggravation, the world would be full of saints.

859

Tsevishen yidden vert men nit farfalen.

One does not perish among Jews.

860

Tsores mit yoich iz gringer tsu fartrogen vi tsores on yoich.

Worries are easier to bear with soup than without it.

861

Tsores tsezegen di hartz.

Trouble cuts up the heart.

862

Tsores vi holtz, un mit vos eintsuhaitsen dem oiven iz nito.
*Troubles (as plenty) as firewood, but you can't heat the oven
with them.*

863

Tsores vil men nit tsunemen; mitsves ken met nit tsunemen.
*Nobody is willing to take away your troubles; nobody can take
away your good deeds.*

864

Tsores zeinen shtarkeh tropens, es toig nit a sach mit a mol.
Trouble is like strong medicine—too much at a time is harmful.

865

Tsu fil anives iz a halber shtoltz.
Too much modesty is half conceit.

866

Tsu fil essen un trinken in dales zinken.
Too much eating and drinking leads to poverty.

867

Tsu gut iz umgezunt.
Anything in excess is unhealthy.

868

Tsu hoben gelt iz a guteh zach; tsu hoben dai'eh iber di gelt,
iz noch besser.
*To have money is a good thing; to have a say over the money
is even better.*

869

Tsu fil koved iz a halbeh shand.
Too much glory is half disgrace.

870

Tsu itlechen nei'em lid ken men tsupassen an alten nigen.
To every new song one can find an old tune.

871

Tsu shain iz amol a chissoren.
Too much of anything is undesirable.

872

Tsulib ton kost tomid tei'er.
Trying to please is always costly.

873

Tsum glik badarf men kain chochmeh nit.
You don't have to be wise to be lucky.

874

Tsum guten vert men bald gevoint.
It doesn't take long to get used to good things.

875

Tsum shlimazel muz men oich mazel hoben.
Even for bad luck one needs luck.

876
Tsum shtain zol men klogen nor nit bei zich zol men trogen.
Better pour out your troubles to a stone, but don't carry them within yourself.

877
Tsum shtarben darf men kain luach nit hoben.
No calendar is needed for dying.

878
Tsuzogen un lib hoben kost nit kain gelt.
It doesn't cost anything to promise and to love.

879
Tsvai falen tsu last: der nar tsevishen klugeh un der kluger tsevishen naronim.
Two are embarrassed: the fool in the company of wise men and the wise man in the company of fools.

880
Tsvai kabtzonim kenen kain ain shabbes nit machen.
Two beggars together cannot afford to prepare for one Sabbath.

881
Tsvai mol a yor iz shlecht dem oreman: zumer un vinter.
Twice a year the poor are badly off: summer and winter.

882
Umglik bindt tsunoif.
Misfortune binds together.

883

Umzist krigt men nor mist.

Only refuse is to be gotten free.

884

Untergenumen haist zich farkoift.

Pledge yourself and you've sold yourself.

885

Vainiker a vort, abi dem emess.

A word less, as long as it's the truth.

886

Varf nit arois di shmutsikeh aider du host di raineh.

Don't throw away the soiled until you have the clean.

887

Veiber hoben nein mos raid.

Women have nine measures of talk.

888

Vellen zein kliger fun alleh iz di gresteh narishkeit.

Trying to outsmart everybody is the greatest folly.

889

Vemen Got vil erkvicken, kenen mentshen nit dershticken.

Whom God wishes to succor, men cannot destroy.

890

Ven a ferd volt gevust vi klain der mentsh iz akegen im, volt
er im doires geven.
*If a horse knew how small a man is compared to it, it would
trample him.*

891

Ven a shikker hot nit kain bronfen redt er chotsh fun bronfen.
*When a drunkard has no whiskey, he will at least talk of
whiskey.*

892

Ven a shlimazel koilet a hon, gait er; drait er a zaiger, shtait
er!
*When a luckless fool kills a rooster, it still hops; when he winds
a clock, it stops!*

893

Ven a yosem leidt, zet kainer nit; ven er frait zich, zet di
gantseh velt.
*When an orphan suffers, nobody notices; when he rejoices, the
whole world sees it.*

894

Ven ain zelner volt gevust vos der anderer tracht, volt kain
krig nisht geven.
*If one soldier knew what the other thinks, there would be no
war.*

895

Ven alleh mentshen zollen tsien oif ain zeit, volt zich di velt ibergekert.

If all men pulled in one direction, the world would topple over.

896

Ven der man iz a balagoleh, hot er nit moireh far di veib's kloleh.

When the husband is a coachman, he is not afraid of his wife's curses.

897

Ven der nar volt nit geven mein, volt ich oich gelacht.

If the fool did not belong to me, I would also laugh.

898

Ven di avaireh iz zis, iz nit bitter di t'shuveh.

When the sin is sweet, the repentance is not bitter.

899

Ven di kalleh iz oif der tseit, kuken di mechutonim on a zeit.

When the bride is expecting, the wedding guests look away.

900

Ven di licht iz krum, iz der shoten krum.

When the light is crooked, the shadow is crooked.

901

Ven di maidel iz aidel, iz di veibel a teibel.

When the girl is refined, the wife is a little dove.

902

Ven di katz shloft, tantsen di meiz.
When the cat is asleep, the mice dance around.

903

Ven di oigen ze'en nit, tut nit vai di hartz.
When the eyes don't see, the heart doesn't ache.

904

Ven di veib trogt di hoizen, vasht der man di spodnitzen.
When the wife wears the pants, the husband washes the floor.

905

Ven di veib vil, az der man zol zein in shtub, redt zi vainiker
un gist vasser mer.
*When the wife wants the husband to stay at home, she talks
less and cleans more.*

906

Ven dos hartz iz bitter, helft nit kain tsuker.
When the heart is bitter, sugar won't help.

907

Ven dos mazel kumt, shtel im a shtul.
If fortune calls, offer him a seat.

908

Ven es felt puter tsu broit, iz es noch nit kain noit.
When you lack butter for the bread, it is not yet poverty.

909

Ven es flit arein der hunger durch der tir, flit arois di libeh durchen fenster.
When hunger slips in through the door, love flies out through the window.

910

Ven es gait gleich, vert men reich.
When things go right, you become rich.

911

Ven es vakst der teister, vaksen di baderftikaiten.
As the wallet grows, so do the needs.

912

Ven es zol helfen Got betten, volt men shoin tsugedungen mentshen.
If it would help to pray to God, then people would be hiring others to pray for them.

913

Ven frait zich a hoiker? Ven er zet a gresseren hoiker far zich.
*When does a hunchback rejoice? When he sees one with a
larger hump.*

914

Ven frait zich an oreman? Ven er farlirt un gefint.
*When does a poor man rejoice? When he has lost something
and found it again.*

915

Ven frait zich Got? Az an oreman gefint a metsieh un git es op.
*When does God rejoice? When a poor man finds a treasure and
returns it.*

916

Ven hungert a nogid? Ven der doktor haist im!
*When does a wealthy man go hungry? When the doctor orders
him.*

917

Ven me lacht ze'en alleh; ven me vaint zet kainer nisht.
When you laugh, all see; when you cry, no one sees.

918

Ven me zol Got danken far guts, volt nit zein kain tseit tsu
baklogen zich oif shlechts.
*If we thanked God for the good things, there wouldn't be time
to weep over the bad.*

919

Ven men darf hoben moi'ach, helft nit kain koi'ach.
When brains are needed, brawn won't help.

920

Ven men fort arois vaist men, ven men kumt tsurik vaist men nit.
We know when we start out; when we'll return, we know not.

921

Ven men hot an ainikel, hot men tsvai kinder.
When you have a grandchild, you have two children.

922

Ven men lebt fun der pushkeh iz laidik di kishkeh.
When one lives out of the alms box, his stomach remains empty.

923

Ven nit di moireh, volt geven zis di avaireh.
If not for the fear of punishment, it would be sweet to sin.

924

Ven nit di shaineh maidlech, volt men gehat dem yaitzer-horeh in der'erd.
If not for pretty girls, temptation would be unheeded.

925

Ven nit di shein, volt kain shoten nit geven.
If not for the light, there would be no shadow.

926

Ven s'farleshen zich di licht, haiben on tantsen di meiz.
When the lights go out, the mice begin to dance.

927

Ven tsores laigt zich nit oifen ponem, laigt zich es oifen hartsen.
When distress doesn't show on the face, it lies on the heart.

928

Ven tsu a krenk iz do a refueh, iz dos a halbeh krenk.
When there's a remedy for an ailment, it's only half an ailment.

929

Ven tsvai shpilen, muz ainer gevinen un ainer farliren.
When two play a game, there must be a winner and a loser.

930

Ver es darf hengen vert nisht dertrunken.
He who is destined to hang won't drown.

931

Ver es hot di hak, git dem k'nak.
He who has the ax gives the whacks.

932

Ver es hot di matbai'eh, der hot di dai'eh.
He who has the money has the authority.

933

Ver es hot gegeben tsain, der vet geben broit.
He who has given teeth, will give bread.

934

Ver es hot gelt hot di gantseh velt!
He who has money has the whole world!

935

Ver es hot lib di melocheh iz im leicht di melocheh.
He who likes his work, to him work comes easy.

936

Ver es kon kain pulver nit shmeken, der zol in der malchumeh nit gai'en!
He who cannot stand the smell of gunpowder should not engage in war!

937

Ver es lacht fun an oreman, der vet veren oif gelechter.
He who laughs at the poor will become the butt of others' jokes.

938

Ver es poret zich mit staleh, shmirt zich ein di hent.
If you deal with tar, expect your hands to get dirty.

939

Ver es toig nit far zich, der toig nit far yenem.
He who is no good to himself is no good to another.

940

Ver es varft oif yenem shtainer krigt tsurik in di aigeneh bainer.

He who throws stones on another gets them back on his own bones.

941

Ver es vert umzist baroiges, vert umzist vider gut.

He who becomes angry for no reason becomes friendly again for no reason.

942

Ver shemt zich fun zeineh mishpocheh, oif dem iz kain brocheh.

Whoever is ashamed of his family will have no luck.

943

Verem essen toiterhait un deiges lebedikerhait.

Worms eat you up when dead and worries eat you up alive.

944

Verter muz men vegen un nit tsailen.

Words must be weighed and not counted.

945

Vest vellen zich oisfeinen far leit, vestu shtarben far der tseit.

If you want to please everybody, you'll die before your time.

946

Vi ainer iz tsu ziben, azoi iz er tsu zibetsik.

As one is at seven, so is he at seventy.

947

Vi dem klugen iz bitter iz der nar alts frailech.
What a wise man bewails, makes the fool happy.

948

Vi me bet zich ois, azoi darf men shlofen.
As you make your bed, so will you sleep in it.

949

Vi men iz gevoint oif der yugend, azoi tut men oif der elter.
That which is practiced in youth will be pursued in old age.

950

Vi zaif faren guf iz a trer far di neshomeh.
Like soap for the body, so are tears for the soul.

951

Vibald du farshtaist dein narishkeit, bistu a kluger!
As long as you understand your foolishness, you are smart!

952

Vildeh grozen vaksen iber nacht.
Crabgrass grows overnight.

953

Voil iz dem vos hot nit kain gelt tsu borgen zeineh freint; er
shaft zich nit kain soinim.
*He is well off who has no money to lend to friends; he doesn't
create enemies.*

954

Voil tsu dem mentshen vos baglikt oif der elter.

Fortunate is the man who has a happy old age.

955

Volt der mentsh nor azoi fil vert geven, vi Got ken helfen.

If only man would deserve as much as God can help.

956

Vos a kind zol nit der'raiden, vet di muter im farshtain.

Whatever a child babbles, its mother will understand.

957

Vos a nar kon kalyeh machen, konen tsen chachomim nit farrichten.

What a fool can spoil, ten wise men cannot repair.

958

Vos a toiber derhert nit, dos tracht er zich ois.

What a deaf man doesn't hear, he imagines.

959

Vos bei a nichteren oif dem lung, iz beim shikker oif der tsung.

What a sober man thinks, a drunkard speaks.

960

Vos der mentsh ken alts ibertrachten, ken der ergster soineh im
nit vintshen.
What a man thinks up for himself, his worst enemy couldn't
wish for him.

961

Vos di oig zet nit, di hartz fielt nit.
What the eye doesn't see, the heart doesn't feel.

962

Vos Got tut basheren, ken kain mentsh nit farveren.
What God decrees, man cannot prevent.

963

Vos Got tut, iz mistomeh gut.
What God does is probably for the best.

964

Vos iz billik iz tei'er.
Cheapest is dearest.

965

Vos me hot, vil men nit; un vos me vil, hot men nit.
What one has, one doesn't want; and what one wants, one
cannot have.

966

Vos mer gevart, mer genart.
He who hesitates is lost.

967

Vos oif der lung, dos oif der tsung.
What's on his mind, is on his tongue.

968

Vos toig shainkeit on mazel?
What use is beauty without good luck?

969

Vos tsu iz iberik.
Too much is superfluous.

970

Vos tsu iz umgezunt.
Excess is unhealthy.

971

Vos vainiker me ret, iz als gezunter.
The less you talk, the better off you are.

972

Vos vintsiker me fregt, iz als gezunter.
The less you ask, the healthier.

973

Vu honik, dort fligen.
Where there is honey, there flies gather.

974
Vu Toireh, dort iz chochmeh.
Where there is knowledge of the Scriptures, there is wisdom.

975
Vu me darf moyech, helft nit kain koyech.
Where you need intellect, strength will not do.

976
Vu sholom, dort iz brocheh.
Where there is peace, there is blessing.

977
Yedeh hartz hot soides.
Every heart has secrets.

978
Yeden dacht zich az bei yenem lacht zich.
One always thinks that others are happy.

979
Yeder barg-aroif hot zein barg-arop.
Every way up has its way down.

980
Yeder mentsh hot zein peckel.
Every man has his burden.

981

Yeder mentsh hot zein aigeneh meshugass.
Every person has his own idiosyncrasies.

982

Yeder mentsh iz oif zich alain blind.
Every man is blind to his own faults.

983

Yeder mentsh vaist az er vet shtarben, ober kainer vil es nisht gloiben.
Every man knows he will die but no one wants to believe it.

984

Yeder morgen brengt zich zorgen.
Every day brings forth its own sorrows.

985

Yedeh mutter denkt ir kind iz shain.
Every mother thinks her child is beautiful.

986

Yeder vaist vu se drikt im der shuch.
Everyone knows where his shoe pinches.

987

Zai shtimen vi a katz un a hunt.
They agree like cat and dog.

988

Zicher iz men nor miten toit.
One is certain only of death.

989

Alleh shlosser ken men efenen mit a goldenem shlissel.
All locks can be opened with a golden key.

990

An einredenish iz erger vi a krenk.
An imaginary illness is worse than a real one.

991

As a laib shloft, los im shlofen!
Let sleeping lions lie!

992

Az me est chazzer, zol men essen fetten.
If you're going to eat pork, let it be good and fat.

993

Az me laight zich in klei'en, shlepen di chazzerim.
He who lies in the sty will be eaten by the pigs.

994

Besser dos besteh fun dem ergsten aider dos ergsteh fun dem besten.
Better the best of the worst than the worst of the best.

995

Fil meloches, vainik broches.
Jack of all trades, master of none.

996

Tachrichim macht men on keshenes.
Shrouds are made without pockets.

997

Fun fartrikenteh baimer kumen kain paires nit arois.
No fruit falls from withered trees.

998

Bist a botu'ach, ober shik arein m'zumonim!
I trust you, but send cash!

999

Ain mol iz geven a chochmeh.
A trick is clever only once.

1000

Ain sheitel holtz macht nit varem dem oiven.
A single log doesn't warm the fireplace.

1001

Altsding lozt zich ois mit a gevain.
Everything ends in weeping.